# MAHAN KHALSA

# LET'S GET REAL

# or Let's Not Play

The Demise of Dysfunctional Selling and the Advent of

## Helping Clients Succeed

**Chapters and Topics**    iii

**Acknowledgments**    ix

Printed by White Water Press

A Rambunctious, Entrepreneurial Division at Franklin Covey Co.

Library of Congress Cataloging-in-Publication Data

Khalsa, Mahan

Let's Get Real or Let's Not Play: The Demise of Dysfunctional Selling and the Advent of Helping Clients Succeed / Mahan Khalsa

p.      cm.

ISBN  1-883219-50-7-73111

1. Selling 2. Business Development 3. Consulting

Book Design by Blaine C. Lee, blaineWorks Graphic Design

© Tony Stone Images: pgs. 1–38, pgs. 49–150, pgs. 183–230
© The Image Bank: pgs. 39–48, pgs. 151–182
© PhotoDisc: pg. 24

# Chapters and Topics

# Acknowledgments

Everything I know about the topics in this book I have learned from someone or somewhere. Acknowledging every contribution would be a book itself. I guess the bad news is that for each person I mention, I leave out dozens more. The good news is that no one reads the acknowledgements anyway, except you, of course. Therefore, I've decided to strip it down to a bare few.

My wife, Mahan Kaur Khalsa, is my greatest teacher. Though I am a poor student, she has taught me much about honest, open, and meaningful communication. For me, she has managed to open a heart in what used to be only intellect and willpower. She would never be in front of a group of people sharing what she knows. However, one on one, people share their deepest thoughts, feelings, aspirations, and difficulties with safety and illumination.

Bob Elmore, as worldwide head of Arthur Andersen's Business Systems Consulting (now Business Consulting), nurtured and sponsored the initial research and application of the early versions of this work. He was a mentor, guide, taskmaster, and friend. As a man of models, vision, and energy, he was willing to commit intellectual, emotional, and business capital to something he believed in. I am very grateful.

Dr. Gurucharan Khalsa, a brilliant man, coauthored a book called *Asking Effective Questions*, and allowed me to participate in researching and developing a body of work called "The Leading Edge Consultant." That time was seminal to this work.

I spent 22 years as the director of a residential community based on the practice of yoga and meditation. Much of what I can offer today comes from what I was granted during that experience. I remain thankful to all of my teachers, friends, and students for what they shared.

Richard Carlson contributed directly to models and skills in this book. Over a several-year period, we worked jointly with major clients. We have enjoyed epiphanies, dialogues, and debates. I know this material is effective because together with Richard, we have lived it, and it has served our clients and us very well. To that end, I also thank all those who teach this material and help it to evolve. They put themselves on the line every day in an attempt to radically improve the way people interact at the interface of business development. They know in the fibers of their being what it means to "get real," and offer continual feedback on what's working and what isn't.

This book would not be physically possible without the considerable talent and efforts of Steve Smith, a colleague at Franklin Covey. For every one part of my efforts, Steve has put in five.

Lastly, I deeply thank all of the organizations and individuals who allowed me to work with them. They shared their models of the world, business and otherwise, from which I have learned tremendously. They shared a willingness to leave their comfort zones and stretch their abilities to help clients succeed, and I wish them continued insight and success.

—Mahan Khalsa

# 1
# The Demise of 20<sup>th</sup> Century Selling

## My Introduction to 20<sup>th</sup> Century Selling

My first encounters with twentieth-century selling were painful. I was working my way through college and needed a job. I took a position as a door-to-door salesman. The person who trained me made it look easy. He had a great territory and when he knocked on the door, people would say, "John—good to see you. What do you have for me today?" I thought to myself, "I can do *this*!" Of course, I was assigned to the worst part of town. I would knock on the door and people would pull down their shades or scream epithets at me. The routine was: knock on the door, get rejected, repeat for 50 to 100 times to get a sale. That was my process. And then when I finally did make a sale, I would have to deliver it a week later only to find no one home, they didn't have money, they didn't live there any more…whatever. It was brutal. It hurt bad.

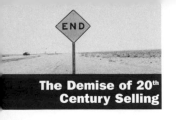

So I took another sales position. It was also door-to-door, and in a city with lots of tall apartment buildings. I figured I could get my rejections more efficiently. All the buildings had skull and crossbones on them that communicated death (and worse) to solicitors. The person who trained me consoled me with the two most repeated words of salespeople: "No problem!" He'd ring the top floor of an apartment building. The person would answer and he'd say, "Western Union!" They'd ring the buzzer and we'd trudge up to the top floor. The person would open the door and my supervisor would begin his pitch. After a couple minutes the person would look confused and say, I thought you were Western Union. My fearless leader would respond, "Western Union? Oh, my goodness. I'm sorry. I said my name is Lester Newman!" The person would slam the door in our faces and we would proceed to work our way through the building.

Needless to say, one of the happiest days of my life was when I got a job in a factory. What bliss! I promised myself that I'd never be involved in sales again. I now knew first-hand how abusive it was to both buyer and seller. Both were sullied.

Later on, much to my surprise, I found myself the director of a residential spiritual community. We arose at 3:30 a.m. each day and did 2½ hours of yoga and meditation—the basis of our practice. We started our own businesses so we could apply our discipline and values in our daily activities. As our community grew, and as our families grew, our needs grew. I was sacrificed to the god of capitalism and sent to a local business school to get an M.B.A. We developed bigger

and more sophisticated businesses. And lo and behold, we had to sell products and services. Ahhhhhh! What a conundrum. As an overly responsible type, I had the impression that if there wasn't enough revenue, it was up to me to bring it in. And as a leader, I needed and wanted to live the values we learned and taught.

Dynamic tension is sometimes the cauldron of creativity. I was motivated to seek out any source that would aid my quest for a highly effective yet mutually respectful means of what I used to call selling. I proceeded to do so aggressively. The combination was tricky. There were times I felt very honorable—and failed miserably. There were times I was successful in getting immediate revenue—and compromised my values and probably my long-term relationship with the customer. There were times I thought I had it all together—and still fell flat on my face. So everything I offer here was born as much from failure as success. I have learned well from both, and offer the current state of affairs in this book.

## The Problem

With due respect to true sales professionals, the notion of sales and selling carries a lot of negative baggage. It is the second oldest profession, often confused with the first. No matter what you put in front or in back of the word "selling" (consultative, solution, visionary, creative, integrity, value-based, beyond), it still ends up with the sense of doing something "to" somebody rather than "for" or "with" somebody.

As it has developed, sales has often become a fear-based relationship. Customers are afraid that they will be "sold" a bill of goods. They fear that a salesperson will talk them into something that is not really right for them. Through lack of information, they fear they will over-pay or make other foolish decisions. Salespeople fear they won't make the sale. If they "lose" enough sales, they won't make quota, they won't get paid well, and they won't meet the needs of themselves and the people important to them. They fail.

Another aspect of a negative sales impression is when salespeople don't help customers get what they want. How tremendously frustrating it is when we actually want to buy something and we can't get adequate help to make a good decision. Even some of the world's largest corporations have, at times, developed a reputation for sales-people who are illusive, ignorant, and arrogant. You can't get them to talk to you; and when they do, they don't really understand your needs, and worse—they don't care.

Clearly this is not true for everyone. There are people (and organizations) who have transcended dysfunctional sales practices and excel at helping people get what they want or need in a way they appreciate. We value these professionals so much, particularly in contrast to what we've come to expect. Toward the end of the twentieth century, several individuals, authors, teachers, and mentors have contributed to breaking the mold, changing the game, and creating a new dynamic between purchasers and providers. I applaud their efforts and would like to add to their efforts.

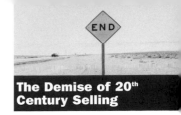

## A Vicious, Downward Cycle

Dysfunctional buying practices have arisen to combat dysfunctional selling practices. Companies send out requests for proposals that, under penalty of dismemberment and death, refuse to allow any human being to talk to any other human beings. They ask us to fill out hundreds of questions, whether they seem relevant or not. Their problems have been developing over years, and they want you to respond in two weeks. Don't do anything different from what they tell you to do, or you are disqualified. And don't differentiate yourself; they want you to follow the rules. They say they want to keep a level playing field. If you have questions, if you want to better understand their needs, it's all in the RFP. Put your questions in writing and they will distribute the answers to everyone. Or go to the bidder's conference and ask your questions in front of all your competitors. The prospective purchasers will stand at a distance, hear what you say, and apart—in their chambers of secrecy—reach their decision. Perhaps they will inform you.

And providers have learned that many requests for their involvement aren't real. The client has no intent to hire them. The client wants to check out prices and see what is happening in the marketplace. They know who they are hiring, but are required to have four bids. They have no qualms whatsoever in having your company spend huge amounts of time, people hours, and money with no real hope of having a working relationship. Some clients have even come to the conclusion that they don't have to pay for services. They just put out an

RFP to five or six companies, have each one explain at length what they would do and how they would do it, then take the best of what they heard and do it themselves. Free consulting!

Buyers don't trust sellers, so they hide and protect vital information and remove personal contact. Sellers have to guess, and often guess wrong. Buyers prove themselves right and create higher hurdles. Sellers acquiesce or try more outlandish gambits. And so it goes.

## What Will Force Us to Change?

There are two powerful forces changing the dynamics of twentieth-century selling: information and global competition.

### Information

The Internet is nascent, and is already radically affecting how people buy. Take one of the true symbols of dysfunctional selling—buying cars. With perfect information, buyers will no longer have to put up with, "Let me talk to my manager," or, "What can I do to get you into this car today?" Through the Internet, many of the fears caused by lack of information are eliminated or reduced.

The impact of "perfect" information (it's never perfect) is stunning. It means that for all products and services perceived to be a commodity, margins will be driven toward zero. Software agents will comb the net seeking the lowest price. If you can't differentiate your services and products, they will be commoditized. If you try to differentiate yourself by selling through human beings, your costs will be higher. The

resulting margins must cover those costs, and if you fail in differentiation, you have more to lose. Sellers of products and services who risk being commoditized have tough choices in choosing a selling strategy.

What should sellers of commodities do? Other than become the low-cost producers (making the acquisition processes easier or more enjoyable) or decommoditizing (changing the game) I don't have an easy answer. We choose to work with companies whose business depends on the enhanced communication and critical thinking skills of human beings. Everybody has a niche—a strength—and that's ours.

## Global Competition

What about noncommodity selling? What is forcing a change there? True global competition. What works succeeds; what doesn't is penalized. Please feel free to hold on to your economic, political, social, and moral philosophies. If they make you effective, you'll prosper—if not, you'll suffer. No country or company is immune. I'm not saying this is good or bad…it just is.

The implication to the sales role is that you *must* help your client succeed. If you do, you both win. If not, you both lose. That's a big switch. It is no longer sufficient to get them to buy. If you can't reduce their costs; increase revenues or margins; leverage their cost of capital; increase productivity, quality, and customer satisfaction; augment a key strategy or initiative; and increase critical performance, you cannot earn their business over time. And if you can't help them achieve sustainable results, you will be a one-time player rather than

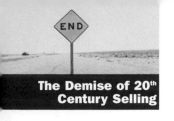
a long-term business partner. One-time players don't stay in business. In the 1980s, U.S. companies were hurting. Everything Japanese was praised. American companies had to radically revise their businesses in order to compete. In the 1990s, that trend reversed. For a long time, IBM was a business idol. Then in the late '80s, they lost 75 percent of their market value. In the '90s, they had to make core changes to come back. Companies like Intel and Microsoft are famed for their "paranoia"—if you don't constantly move ahead, you'll fall behind. No one can take anything for granted in today's rapidly changing, highly competitive global marketplace.

As a business person, I can't afford to give business to Fred because he's my golf partner. I can't stand pat with XYZ just because I've done business with them for 10 years. I don't have time for a lot of chitchat and sales pitches, or poorly designed schemes. Let's cut to the chase and cut through the nonsense. Let's get real. Whomever I'm working with has to keep growing *their* abilities to grow *my* abilities. I have to get better, or I'm getting worse; the people with whom I'm working will have to help me get better. Oh, and by the way, it better be fun. I want to enjoy the process. Life is too short, too precious, and I have choices.

## What Will Allow Us to Change?

People (including me) have been doing the best they can with twentieth-century sales models. Yet those models have fundamental flaws. My belief and experience is that if people have a better model, better skills, *and* if they get better results, they will change. Otherwise they

will fall back on what they know, even if it seems dysfunctional. My goal is to contribute both to a new model and to the skills that make the model effective. Since I like to practice what I preach—walk my talk—I get to be an everyday laboratory to see what works and what doesn't. Since I am in a position to share the model with others, the model grows stronger as many people contribute better distinctions and improved applications.

Gandhi said, "Let us be the change we want to see in the world." Change is ultimately an individual choice. I choose to change. I have sold to survive ("I've got to get some sales"), I have sold out of ego ("I can get them to do this"), and I have helped clients succeed. I know the difference in my body, mind, heart, and gut. What I am most thankful for is that helping clients succeed not only feels so much better, it is tremendously more effective. If it weren't more effective, I would have difficulty holding on to the model or sharing it with anyone else.

## Helping Clients Succeed

Helping clients succeed is not a euphemism for sales or selling. It is a paradigm, a mental model, a frame of reference, a methodology for two or more companies to work together for mutual success and satisfaction. If that sounds corny, so be it. It is based on much research, development, and real-world testing. Take what resonates as common sense, even if it is not common application. Use what works for both you and the people you work with. Leave the rest behind. Better yet, help improve the model based on your experience.

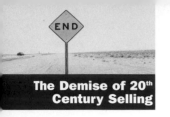
## Awareness and Choice

Even though there is a lot of dysfunction in business development, there are clearly some things that do work—that provide mutual success. *If you're doing something that's getting you the results you want, keep doing it.* There is no single, ultimate sales methodology or way of doing things that brings optimal results in all situations.

The goal is to augment your awareness of what's really possible to accomplish in business development dialogues, and increase your choices about how to succeed in a mutually beneficial way. So, rather than absolute right or wrong, good or bad, black or white, we're going to talk about awareness and choice. Everything I offer in this book needs your awareness of when it does or doesn't make sense, and intelligent choices in application. Using awareness and choice will also be the most liberating way to approach our clients. Rather than giving them ultimatums, dogmas, and platitudes, we need to give them expanded awareness of possibilities and superior choices— help them make good business decisions in their own best interest.

## Disclaimer

This book is only an overview of a body of work. It is not meant as a textbook or a "how to." It is based on research and in-person training sessions given around the world. If you have taken the training, it can serve as a review. If you haven't taken the training, it can help you decide whether or not to bother. This book doesn't accomplish what can happen human being to human being.

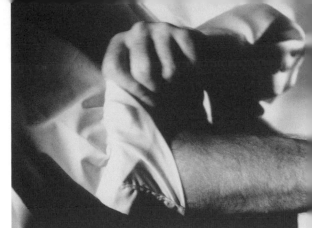

# 2
# Definition of Terms

Before we get started, allow me to define some terms used throughout
the book.

**Client.** I use this term to mean *anyone* whom we are trying to help
succeed. It doesn't matter if they have purchased our products or
services. Even if this is our first dialogue, they are a client; I am trying
to help them get what is important to them whether it is with me or
not. The client could be internal or external. Importantly, the client
could be multiple people—and often is. Please read into the context
of the usage a meaning that seems appropriate for you.

**Consultant.** I use this term to mean anyone trying to help a client
succeed. It could be a salesperson, a business developer, a consultant, a technical advisor, or a friend. It could be multiple people.

Again, please read into the context of the usage a meaning that seems appropriate for you.

**Helping clients succeed:** helping people and organizations achieve what is important to them in a way they feel good about. It is a paradigm, mental model, or frame of reference for how consultants work effectively with clients.

**Getting "real":** a subjective term, meaning different things to different people. It is used in this book to mean to be authentic; to be truthful; to say what you mean; to be congruent with what you value; to penetrate past lazy thinking, facades, games, defenses, fears, illusions; to get a core understanding; to get to the heart of the matter; to open your belief systems to examination; to increase your awareness of what is really going on, and your choices of how to respond.

**It is reasonable to have perfection in our eye that we may always advance toward it, though we know it can never be reached.**

*Samuel Johnson*

**Exact solution.** No solution is exact or perfect—there is no such thing. It is, at best, an asymptotic relationship—we come closer and closer, but never get there completely. I use exact solution to stand for the idea of a solution that truly, or most closely, meets the client's needs.

*Note: The next five chapters will focus on the principles of communication and critical thinking that are essential to effective business development. Following those chapters, we will apply those principles to the process (ORDER) of business development.*

# 3
# We Both Want the Same Thing

I have some good news and some bad news.

## The Good News

We and our clients share identical, mutual self-interests: we both
want the same thing. We both want a solution that truly meets the
client's needs. From our own, selfish perspective, why would *we* want
that? If the client doesn't perceive they are getting a solution that truly
meets their needs, they can choose to go somewhere else. If enough
clients make that choice, we start hurting. However, not buying from
us is not the worst that can happen. Worse is if they buy our solution
and then figure out it doesn't meet their needs. Then we either spend
all of our profits and more trying to make it right, or we have an
unhappy client. Everyone has seen the statistics on how many good
clients it takes to overcome one dissatisfied client. So from our per-

spective, if the client doesn't think they are getting a solution that truly meets their needs, we lose.

What about the client? If they don't perceive there is a solution that meets their needs, they don't buy it. All the problems they were hoping to solve go unsolved. All the results they hoped to achieve go unattained. If they do buy it and it doesn't meet their needs, they waste all the solution-acquisition costs, they incur implementation costs, they still forgo the expected economic benefits, and each additional attempt to get a solution meets with more cynicism, resistance, and less likelihood of success.

We both want the same thing. We both want a solution that truly meets the client's needs. It is win-win if we get it, it is lose-lose if we don't. I think that's good news. Knowing we both want the same thing should make the task easier.

## The Bad News

The bad news is that clients don't consistently get a solution that meets their needs. Even though both of us want it, even though we both lose if it doesn't happen, both we and the client engage in counterproductive behaviors. Let's look at some of those behaviors to increase our awareness of what happens on both sides. With awareness comes an opportunity for the choice of something better.

**We Both Want the Same Thing**

## Consultants

When I ask consultants what they do that inhibits getting a solution which truly meets the client's needs, here are some of the things they tell me:

- We don't listen.
- We make assumptions.
- We have preconceived solutions.
- We need to make the sale.
- It takes too much time.
- We don't understand their business.
- We know what they need better than they do.
- We don't talk to the right people.

## Clients

What about the clients? You know they want a solution that really meets their needs, yet what do they do? This is what I hear:

- They don't know what they need.
- They can't articulate what they need.
- They don't agree on what they need.
- They won't give us good information.
- They don't let us talk to the right people.
- They are unrealistic about time, money, and people needed.
- Politics count more than business sense.
- They procrastinate.
- They can't make decisions.

Even though we both want the same thing, both of us engage in behaviors that make the goal more difficult.

15

## Three Predictable Approaches

In response to this dynamic, there are three predictable approaches we as consultants use with clients:

### 1. We tell.

This is so much easier than understanding the client. We just tell them what the problem is, what they need to do, and to just do it! Of course, it helps if we have written a book—then we are "qualified" experts. I'm sure you can imagine some situations when telling *may* be an effective and appropriate approach. Yet, what are the downsides of telling?

- We might be wrong. (It is at least a statistical possibility.)
- No buy-in or ownership from the client—which could ensure failure.
- They can put all the blame on us if it fails.
- They see us as arrogant.
- We only get the opportunity we tell them about—and we potentially leave many opportunities uncovered.

### 2. We accept.

The client tells us what they want, and we give it to them. We walk through the door, they write us a check, and we leave. Easy, isn't it? Again, accepting *may* be appropriate. What could possibly go wrong?

- *They* could be wrong (and they will *still* blame us).
- We haven't added any value—any thought leadership.
- We won't understand root causes.
- We could leave many opportunities uncovered.

## 3. We guess.

Of course, we as consultants don't like to call it guessing—we call it diagnosis, assessment, or analysis. If you didn't know better, it would look like guessing. One or two consultants talk to one or two client counterparts for about an hour. Based on that, they start guessing: What do we think they really need? What do we think the true problems are? Why haven't they fixed this before now? What should we propose? Do you think we were talking to the right people? Do you think they have any money to pay for this? How much should we charge? Who do you think the competition is? And so on.

Consultants, being the intelligent people we are, have formalized the guessing process—we call it a proposal. And you can always tell how much we are guessing. The more we guess, the bigger the proposal!

## A Fourth Approach

I'd like to suggest a fourth option: we *mutually explore* with the client the shared outcome of a solution that truly meets their needs—whether with us or someone else. Of course, that's not easy. Clients have come to *expect* that we will tell, accept, and guess. It has become the norm. Even worse, they may try to *force* us to tell (you're the expert), accept (just give us what we want), or guess (it's all in the RFP).

This book is dedicated to the fourth approach of mutual exploration and to the goal of a solution that truly meets the client's needs. It

may not happen every time, and it can happen far more often. And when it can't happen, we can always resort to our best telling, accepting, or guessing.

# 4
# EQ-IQ

## Two Dimensions

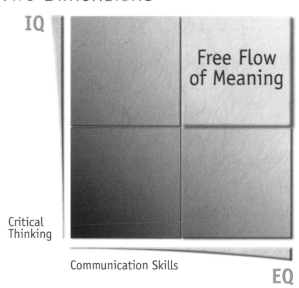

IQ

Free Flow of Meaning

Critical Thinking

Communication Skills

EQ

In helping clients succeed, we work along two dimensions. One dimension is EQ (emotional quotient) and the other is IQ (intelligence quotient). EQ and IQ are major determinants of our ability to get real. EQ is a measure of how well and how fast we can talk openly, human being to human being. High EQ can allow us to get past the games, the roles, the facades, the fears, and honestly share

what we are truly thinking, feeling, and believing—to open our beliefs to discussion. EQ is partly our ability to trust our instinct and emotions, even to the point where we override the input IQ has provided.

IQ is a measure of how effectively we can critically examine our beliefs—how much intellectual rigor we can apply to our analysis. IQ helps us clarify and test our assumptions, presuppositions, and mental models; balance our gut instinct with data; gather evidence and impact for key issues; uncover critical constraints (past, present, and future); apply good tenets of systemic thinking; carefully explore the implications one solution would have on the whole, etc. In essence, are we willing to take a detached, unbiased view of what is really going on? If we continually increase our capacity along both dimensions, we dramatically augment our ability to help clients succeed.

## Intellectual Piranha Versus Warm and Fuzzy

I once interacted with one of the world's top consulting firms. They would eat, drink, and sleep IQ. Some of their own clients described them as "brains on a stick." In their meetings, when they would throw an idea on the table, it was like watching piranhas feed. They would attack and devour the idea, tear it apart, and if anything was left at the end they would say, "Oh, must be a good idea." For them it was a valid form of critical thinking. The problem was, when they tried to use the "piranha process" with their clients, their clients found it tremendously arrogant and obnoxious—and probably intimidating. What worked well as an internal paradigm transferred poorly

to external situations; there was little flexibility to adapt styles to differing requirements. This inflexibility proved a serious challenge as the firm decided to make implementation a major plank of their own strategy. Clients would put up with them for two or three weeks, maybe even for two or three months, but rarely for two or three years. They had to significantly stretch their EQ to help their clients (and themselves) succeed.

I've also worked with companies that were much higher in EQ than IQ. One company in particular had an incredible ability to develop rapport and trust with clients, and they backed that ability with quality content; yet they lacked the intellectual horsepower to really connect their services to business results. This was a serious limitation in helping clients succeed and thus impeded their growth potential. To truly help clients succeed, both IQ and EQ are necessary. Lack of either is a fatal flaw.

## Asking Hard Questions in a Soft Way

Using both EQ and IQ gives us the ability to ask hard questions in a soft way. If we're going to get to solutions that exactly meet our clients' needs, we're going to have to ask some tough questions— questions to which often a little voice in our brain says, "Oh you can't ask that. That's too hard! That would offend them." Our IQ will allow us to know which hard questions need to be asked, and our EQ will allow us to ask in a way that builds rapport with our clients. By not asking at all, we miss the discovery of vital information critical to mutual success.

**EQ-IQ**

# 5
# Intent Counts More Than Technique

If you are going to help your clients succeed, you'll need information from them. To get that information, you'll be asking questions. The intent or purpose for asking questions is a critical determinant of their effectiveness. Your clients are making decisions about what questions are safe to answer. Is the intent of your questions to help them get what they want in a way they feel good about, or to help you get what you want in a way you feel good about? Whose agenda are you on?

> **Who you are stands over you and thunders so I cannot hear what you say.**
>
> *Emerson*

## The Trust Alarm

When you ask a question of your client, that question first gets routed to their brain stem, and to a little place on the brain stem called the amygdala. The amygdala determines flight, fright, or freeze—in other words, survival. So when the question comes in, our brain determines whether it's safe or unsafe. Only if the amygdala says

You can't get access to here...

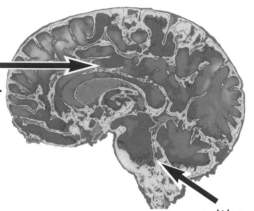

...without first passing the test here.

The intention behind an action determines its effects, every intention affects both us and others, and the effects of intentions extend far beyond the physical world.... It is, therefore, wise for us to become aware of the many intentions that inform our experience, to sort out which intentions produce which effects, and to choose our intentions according to the effects that we desire to produce.

*Gary Zukav,*

THE SEAT OF THE SOUL

safe does the question get rerouted to the neocortex, which is the part of the brain where we think, feel, and believe things to be true. So if clients don't sense that your question is in their best interest, the "trust alarm" will go off and you literally will not gain access to what is "real" to them. You'll get cut off.

The amygdala works largely on pattern recognition based on past experiences. If people have "learned" to mistrust salespeople, and if you look like one, sound like one, and act like one, then to the amygdala, you must be one. *You are guilty until proven innocent.* You can't claim to be innocent. You can't just say, "Trust me," and magically be trusted. You must actually be trustworthy. Most people can't fake intent. It has to be who you are. People have built-in authenticity detectors.

## The "Q" Word

The irony is, the harder you try to "sell" people, the less likely it is going to happen, and the more likely it is that the trust alarm will go off. Once the trust alarm goes off, information flow is curtailed, and you are less likely to get a solution they perceive meets their needs. The more you honestly want to help them succeed, the more likely they are to share their beliefs about what that success is. Consequently, your ability to find the right solution and their trust in adopting it go up as well. It is in our own most selfish interest to focus on the interest of the client first.

Some part of us understands this dynamic. And yet we have this magic word that looms up before us. It starts with a Q, and it's called "quota." So often we're pressured to meet our personal and organizational revenue goals that our intent becomes "Meet the goals! Make the sale!" And perversely, the harder we try, the worse we do. *The more important it is to meet your numbers, the more important it is to stop concentrating on your numbers and start concentrating on your clients' numbers.* If you help them meet their numbers, they will be happy to help you meet yours.

## Create Success Twice

Dr. Stephen R. Covey's work regarding highly effective people revealed that those who are optimal performers create success twice: once in their own mind before it happens, and then once in execution. Can you imagine an Olympic athlete meandering over to the starting

> **One thing we've discovered with certainty is that anything we do that makes the customer more successful, inevitably results in a financial return for us.**
>
> *Jack Welch*

> **The more important it is to meet your numbers, the more important it is to stop concentrating on your numbers and start concentrating on your clients' numbers.**

line of the event and saying, "Oh, it's 10 o'clock. I guess it's time to do my event. Are we about to start? All right, what the heck, let's go." No. When the gun goes off, they're already operating at peak performance. They've already seen what it looks like to perform well. They've heard the crowd cheering as they've gone across the line, and they've felt that experience. They create success twice: once in their own mind before it happens, and then once when it actually transpires.

So get crystal clear about *your* intent before you pick up the phone or walk through that door, because it's going to affect everything else that follows. Make sure it's an intent they can feel is in their best interest. Practice getting connected with that intent so it becomes who you are, not what you say or what you claim; so it communicates before you even say a single word, because that's when people start making that decision.

The decision to trust doesn't start inside them—it starts inside you. Intent is a choice, and your choice will have consequences. You will communicate your intent whether you want to or not. To say it in a grammatically deficient way, you cannot *not* communicate your intent. Based on your intent, people will decide to trust you or not.

The intent I personally choose, and the intent of this process, is to help clients succeed in a way they feel good about. Clearly this is not an altruistic endeavor. We know our products and services have helped clients succeed, or we wouldn't be in business. Clients are hoping we can help them succeed, or they wouldn't invite us in. The

intent to get a solution that exactly meets their needs is a common-sense process designed to increase our success by concentrating first on the success of others. It helps ensure a good fit between what we do and what they need. If there is a good fit, let's work together, have fun, and make money. If not, let's find out quickly, shake hands, and part friends. And if our solution doesn't fit, or they have more pressing needs, maybe we can help them find their solution somewhere else.

## Check Your Ego at the Door

There are thoughts, beliefs, and experiences that will push against the intent we are trying to adopt. We all have an ego (so it seems), and our ego is focused on getting *our* needs met—that's what egos do. So you might imagine that it could take a paradigm shift to convince our ego that our needs will be met more effectively by first meeting the needs of others. We certainly want to maintain all the benefits our ego provides; and yet, because it interferes with clear, objective thinking, it is often helpful (though not easy) to check our ego at the door. We can go get it if needed.  If we can stay aware of its presence and con-sciously choose to leave it aside or employ it, we achieve a major enhancement of both EQ and IQ. If not, our ego can blur the focus.

Our ego can rush in, unbidden, to save us when we are threatened. If you find yourself defending or seeking approval, or demonstrating your brilliance, you are probably serving your needs rather than your client's. Your ego has stepped in. Checking your ego at the door allows you to be fearless, flexible, and to have fun. You can be fearless because you have nothing to lose. You can be totally flexible because

**Intent Counts More Than Technique**

**Clients would rather do business with people who don't need the business.**

you are not attached to any one approach, and are on the client's agenda. The conversation goes where the client needs it to go. Finally, the process can be fun because you are objective. You can enjoy the situation rather than feel pressured to dictate the outcome. Learning to check your ego will afford you emotional independence during business-development situations. And ironically, *clients would rather do business with people who don't need the business.*

## Technique Is Also Important

Technique is also important. You could be the most well-intentioned person in the world, a really fine human being; and if you have no communication skills—no critical-thinking tools—that will not cut it. If that technique doesn't serve your intent, and if that intent doesn't serve the people you're working with, everything else will be limited. I won't say worthless, it will certainly be limited.

# 6
# No Guessing

If our intent is to help clients succeed, we have both the right and the obligation not to guess about the key elements of that success. Guessing and getting real are counterpoised. Getting real is partly defined by our ability to stop guessing and find out what is really going on. We shouldn't guess about what the solution is supposed to solve, how we will measure success, what constraints would impede success, what resources are available to apply toward success, what steps will be involved in the decision process, who will be involved, what criteria they will apply, etc. Our motto is:

## *"No Guessing!"*

**I attribute the little I know to my not having been ashamed to ask for information.**

*John Locke*

No Guessing

## Just Because We Speak the Same Language...

A woman seeking a divorce went to visit her attorney. The first question he asked her was, "Do you have grounds?"

She replied, "Yes, about two acres."

He said, "Perhaps I'm not making myself clear. Do you have a grudge."

She responded, "No, but we have a carport."

Impatiently, he tried again, "Does your husband beat you up?"

She smiled and said, "No, I generally get up before him."

The attorney switched approaches in one last effort, "Ma'am, are you sure you really want a divorce?"

She said firmly, "I don't want one at all, but my husband does. He claims we have difficulty communicating."

*(Pat Swindall, a Georgia Representative, told this story to Congress to show they weren't listening to the public about the deficit.)*

## What Do You Mean?

**The greatest enemy of communication is the illusion of it.**

*Pierre Martineau*

We often mistake fluency (we both use the words easily) with comprehension (we both have the same meanings for the words). Our guess is that because we understand what something means to *us*, it must mean the same to everyone else. We may assume not only that *we* know what they mean, we assume *they* know what they mean, and neither of us may have a clue. Often clients describe their situation with what linguists call "complex equivalents" or "high-level abstractions." These are words or phrases that encode many experiences and beliefs into one small package. Like an iceberg, the word

floats above the surface and the multiple meanings and interpretations lurk below.

To avoid guessing, we need to listen carefully to the key words or phrases clients use, and ask what those words mean to them. It is astounding how often clients come back with something very different than what we expect, or something very useful and valuable.

**The more an organization knows about a term or concept relevant to its business, the less likely it is to agree on a common term or meaning for it.**

*Thomas Davenport,*
INFORMATION ECOLOGY

For example, if you were selling data-warehousing solutions and the client asked if you "did" data warehousing, wouldn't you be tempted to launch into your presentation to powerfully persuade the client that your company had the best solution on the market? Rather than give in to the temptation, what if you were to not guess what the client meant by data warehousing?

Client:         "We are interested in data warehousing. Do you do that?"
Consultant:    "We do. And interestingly enough every client we help

No Guessing

usually has a different sense of what data warehousing means. Do you mind if I ask—when you say data warehousing, what does that mean to you in the context of what you are trying to achieve?"

Now we're not guessing about the meaning, and neither are they. They get a chance to explain themselves and think about what they're trying to achieve, and we get the opportunity to learn more. Instead of mutual mystification, we get mutual understanding.

## NO GUESSING CHALLENGE 1

Write down several words or phrases in your line of business that are commonly used, and for which there are multiple meanings and interpretations. The next 10 times you hear someone say one of those words, promise yourself you will ask the person what he or she means. Keep note of how often people come up with something either very surprising or very useful.

# I Just Assumed...

Assumptions are another form of guessing. They are particularly insidious because they often happen unconsciously; we don't even realize we are guessing. For instance, in business development, we often work with solutions and problems. Dennis Matthies, in his book *Precision Questioning*, takes the following phrase and examines possible assumptions:

*The solution to the problem*

Possible assumptions:

- The problem is real; it exits; it hasn't gone away or wasn't an illusion in the first place. (an existence assumption)
- There is only one problem. Several different problems aren't intertwined. (a uniqueness assumption)
- It is possible to solve the problem. (a possibility assumption)
- The problem has only one solution. (uniqueness)
- The situation a "problem" suggests has a value assumption. Having a problem is bad; having a solution would be good.
- People care about the problem. (value)
- We can measure the extent of the problem. (a measurement assumption)
- Different people perceive the problem the same. (existence, value, measurement)
- It is possible to determine if the solution is valid. (measurement)
- The solution would solve the entire problem. (possibility, measurement)

> When we listen to someone talk, the brain is constantly making assumptions—hundreds of them. Each word, gesture, inflection, and tone of voice is interpreted, but not always as the speaker intended. We usually are not aware of the fact that we are selecting one meaning from a number of possibilities.
>
> *Paul Swets*

- The cost of the solution is less than the cost of the problem. (value, measurement)

- The solution wouldn't cause more problems, or a worse problem.

- The solution will be valid over time. (time/constancy)

- Others?

These are, of course, only a sample of the assumptions we make. The goal is to become more aware of what assumptions are present, and make better choices about when and how to question them.

## NO GUESSING CHALLENGE 2

After your next meeting with a client (phone or face-to-face), take a few minutes to write down all of the assumptions that went unchallenged. How many might be critical? Repeat the procedure for at least five interactions.

## The Question We Never Ask

Often a question forms in our mind and, for whatever reason, we don't ask it. We then have to guess about the answer. Rather than guess, often about critical information, we need both the courage and consideration to ask the question.

For instance, the client says, "You should know that the budget is very limited for this project." Have you heard a response like this before: "Great, and thanks for letting us know; that shouldn't be a problem because our prices are the best in the business"? And what wasn't asked? What that limited budget was. The client's limited budget may have been more than we ever imagined. So we guess about what they are willing and able to spend, and they guess about how much it is going to cost. Neither of us usually finds out anything until we present our proposal. And by then, if our guesses are far off (and they probably are), we may have grossly wasted each other's time.

Much of the discipline recommended and to be followed in this process is to listen to the questions forming in your mind and then find an appropriate (high EQ) way to ask them. Even if it seems inappropriate to you (or uncomfortable), if your intent is aligned with your counterpart, ask the question!

**I am prejudiced in favor of him who, with impudence, can ask boldly. He has faith in humanity and faith in himself. No one who is not accustomed to giving grandly can ask nobly and with boldness.**

*Johann Kaspar Lavater*

No Guessing

## NO GUESSING CHALLENGE 3

In your next several conversations, personal or professional, make a conscious effort to ask the questions you find yourself hesitating to ask. Keep a log of the questions you still refuse to ask. Is there a pattern? What is stopping you? What would have to happen before you would ask the question? Could you find a low-risk opportunity to try?

## What Do They *Really* Expect?

It is fascinating to watch consultants and salespeople make presentations to potential clients whose criteria are unknown to them. They even guess about the very criteria the client will use to evaluate their proposed solutions or findings. It seems many consultants present to the criteria that makes the most sense to them rather than finding out what would make most sense to the client. *Never make a presentation or proposal to people whose criteria for judging you are unknown to you.* To do that would be immense guessing, and we are trying to maintain a relationship of mutual understanding. In other words…no guessing!

> **Judge a man by his questions, not by his answers.**
>
> *Voltaire*

> **Never make a presentation or proposal to people whose criteria for judging you are unknown to you.**

### NO GUESSING CHALLENGE 4

Before you make your next presentation or proposal (of any kind), ask yourself, "Do I really understand the criteria on which I am being judged?" If not, try to find those criteria before presenting your solution.

As we move forward with the business development process, I will note many places where our principle of no guessing applies.

**No Guessing**

# 7
# Slow Down for Yellow Lights

### Three Paradigm Shifts

When you are driving along, particularly when you are anxious to arrive somewhere important, and you encounter a yellow light, what do you do? If you are like most people I know, you go faster. Yellow lights have become the universal symbol for "speed up!" Unfortunately, we use that same response with our clients. We hear something that concerns us, see a reaction that spells potential trouble, feel we are running into difficulty, and we speed up to avoid running into our own worst fears. Ultimately, we are afraid the light will turn red. Our experience in business development has convinced us that hitting a red light is failure, and so when we see yellow, we close our eyes and speed up, hoping we make it through. If we can't slow down for yel-

**Slow Down for Yellow Lights**

low lights, it's hard to get real—either with ourselves, our clients, or the solution.

If hitting a red light is unavoidable, when would we like to hit it? As soon as possible! Intellectually, we know that; emotionally, we resist it. Here are three paradigm shifts that allow us to "manage lights" with our clients effectively:

1. Slow down for yellow lights.
2. A red light is not failure. Failure is making a red light needlessly more expensive (spending a lot more time, money, and company resources to hit the same red light that could have been reached very early in the game).
3. Hand the yellow light to our clients and ask them to turn it to red or green. (Often their criteria for resolution are less stringent than ours. And if they turn it to green, it's far more convincing to them than if we do it.)

During conversations with a client, they will give you signals about how they are feeling and what they are thinking. Those signals will come verbally (what they say to you), vocally (how they say it—their inflection, emphasis, tone, pace), and visually (their nonverbal communication). As a "professional communicator," you'll need the awareness to sense the signals and choose intelligently how to deal with them.

## Damn the Yellow Lights, Full Speed Ahead

Here is an example, with me as the goat. I was calling on a large financial services firm. Because their offices were just a few blocks from another major client of mine, I invited an important partner from a large consulting firm to accompany me—so I could show off my tremendous talents. (That was the first yellow light—I most definitely did not check my ego at the door.) We were supposed to meet with the person championing our cause, the chief executive officer, and a vice president of marketing. When we arrived we were informed my champion wasn't going to be there. He was flying in from out of town. (That was the second yellow light, and I moved right ahead.) As we were escorted up to the offices, we were informed that the CEO also couldn't make the meeting (another *major* yellow light). If I hadn't invited the VIP to accompany me, I might have called off the meeting. I still should have called it off…and didn't.

We then proceeded to meet with the vice president of marketing. At this point I was very angry, upset, and knew I was talking to the wrong person. I proceeded anyway. (My ego would not be checked at any door known to mere mortals.) I did my best to focus on the issues at hand. The vice president was very polite and answered all of my questions, yet every neuron in my body was screaming, "This is going nowhere!" It was a scene resplendent with yellow lights, multiple and flashing.

Had I my wits about me instead of my ego, I would have said something like, "John, you are being very polite and courteous, and yet my intuition is telling me that this is going nowhere, and as soon as I walk out the door, nothing of substance will occur. What are you feeling at this point?" On this particular occasion, I lacked both the clarity and the courage. I said nothing, and sure enough, nothing happened. I wasn't fearless or flexible, and I didn't have fun.

It turned out the vice president had selected another firm in advance, had committed to them, and did everything in his power to make sure I didn't talk to the CEO or anyone else. In retrospect, the competitor's solution did not meet the company's needs. It failed miserably, and the vice president was let go—small solace to my inability to practice what I teach (and what I usually do).

Even if I had slowed down for the yellow lights, there was no guarantee I could have turned them to green; at least I could have been "real" or authentic. I would have had a chance to deal with what was really going on. The move to green or red could have been conscious and participatory rather than passive. Aaahhh…continuous learning.

## The Courage to Say It

On the flip side, I was observing a call by the head of a regional consulting firm to the newly appointed CEO of a highly desirous potential client. This CEO had come from one of the major international consulting firms, who just happened to have offices in the same building. The obvious yellow light was that this large project could go

to the CEO's former firm, and my client would have the wonderful experience of spending lots of money on a proposal that had no chance. He had the courage to say what he was feeling. The conversation went something like this:

**If you see it, hear it, or feel it, find a way to say it—tactfully.**

Consultant:  "Frank, if I were in your shoes, I imagine that I might give preference on this type of a project to people I know and trust, such as my old firm. Have you at all been headed in that direction?"

Potential Client:  "That's certainly a consideration."

Consultant:  "Well let's deal with that head on. What would you have to see or hear or experience from us that would be so compelling that this would be at least a tough choice?"

With some time and skill, the consultant was able to elicit the details that would make a difference, demonstrate them, and win the account.

The rule with yellow lights is: *If you see it, hear it, or feel it, find a way to say it—tactfully.*

## State the Obvious

Your clients will give you signals that will tell you the conversation has hit a yellow light. You can sense when there is not congruence between the words they say and how they say them, how they appear, and how you sense they really feel. Slowing down relies on your

43

**Slow Down for Yellow Lights**

awareness of what is going on and your choices of what to do about it. One very powerful choice is to state the obvious, hopefully without unneeded emotional charge. Here is a three-part response that seems to work well:

1. "I have a concern." (Or, "I am confused." Or, "I think we may have a problem.")
2. State the concern (or the confusion, or the potential problem).
3. Ask what they think should happen next.

Here are some examples of yellow lights and how you can slow down for them effectively:

They request a feature you don't provide.
1. I think we may have a problem.
2. We do everything else you've mentioned and do it well. We don't do X and don't plan to in the near future.
3. What do you think we should do?

They are working with an incumbent.
1. I have a concern.
2. You've been working with XYZ for five years. They're a good company.
3. Why change now?

They may have already decided.
1. I'm getting a feeling I'd like to run by you.
2. With all due respect, and please don't take this personally, I sense

**Slow Down for Yellow Lights**

that no matter how good my proposal is, the decision has already been made.

3. Am I off base?

They seem unwilling to make a financial commitment.

1. I'm confused.
2. You said this project could save tens of millions, yet you are only willing to spend tens of thousands.
3. What am I missing?

Or:

1.  I think we may have a problem.
2. I believe it's really possible to get the results we discussed, though not for the budget you've allocated.
3. What do you think we should do?

A more subtle example might be something like the client glancing at his or her watch continually. You could say: "I noticed you glanced at your watch. Do we have a time constraint?" or "I get the feeling that what I've suggested doesn't really interest you. Are we still on track here, or have we drifted?"

When you ignore yellow lights, they do exactly what yellow traffic lights do: they turn red and you are stopped. Let's get real—or let's not play. Ignoring yellow lights is a form of guessing, and we have committed to *no guessing*.

**Slow Down for Yellow Lights**

## To London and Back

Here's a story of one of the strongest commitments to slowing down for a yellow light that I've seen. One of my clients was working on a very big deal with a company in London. They put four people on a plane in Chicago, business class, and flew to London to meet with them. When they arrived in London, at the last minute the CEO said, "I really apologize, I've got a customer emergency. I've got to fly out and take care of it. Just meet with my team, and they'll fill me in." They knew that was a critical yellow light. If they couldn't get the CEO's buy-in and attendance in the process, they weren't going to get the account at all. They said, "You should attend to your client. If we were your client, we would want that kind of attention. If you were our client we'd want to treat you that way. This project is too important to not have you in the meeting with us. We'll come back when you can meet with us." Four people, business class, got on the plane and flew back to Chicago. They did not have the meeting because they didn't have enough time and the time wasn't right.

That is a fairly extreme example; it does point out what we're talking about. If the client can't focus on and commit their mental energies to what you're doing, and you see and feel the yellow light, then trying to rush through it or make it happen anyway doesn't make much sense.

## Red Lights

Red lights are not bad—they are just red lights. They don't even mean
the opportunity is over. They do mean we hit a deal stopper, which if
unresolved, *will* mean it's over. At least we are aware of what's going
on and can exercise some choices. Remember that a red light is not
failure. If we get it quickly—take our best shot at resolving it, and
can't—we have saved a lot of valuable time. Failure is making red
lights needlessly more expensive.

As we progress through the business development process
(ORDER), we will examine predictable yellow lights and offer some
choices on how to deal with them. If we can't deal with them successfully, then *we* are the ones who may be turning the light to red.
When the client turns the light to red, and we believe it was done
inappropriately, there are some language patterns presented in this
book that will give you more choices.

**Slow Down for Yellow Lights**

# 8
# ORDER

## The Value of a Model

There are a lot of "models" in the world. Every book on management or business seems to have one (or more!). While they are overused in many cases, models can help us take a complex (sometimes even chaotic) series of events and processes, and represent them in an understandable, transferable way. The ORDER model helps balance sophistication with simplicity in business development. Each of the ORDER modules explored in this book is packaged with numerous communication and critical-thinking strategies and skills. Taken as a whole, a consistent application of ORDER increases our ability to create *mutual* success.

## The Limitations of a Model

The cliché here is, "The map is not the territory." The model is not necessarily reality. The model is an abstract of how people develop

business at a high level of expertise. The model is applied in a variety of ways in a variety of situations. Surprisingly, the "what" of the model—it's fundamental premises—has stayed consistent around the world; the "how"—the way in which people apply it—has changed considerably between countries, cultures, cities, industries, solutions, and personalities. And it will change for you.

ORDER is depicted in a linear fashion. In business development (where the model gets real), it ends up being applied in an iterative way. The information that comes from ORD is developed over many conversations, like fitting pieces into a puzzle over time. And even though we try to maintain a strict precedence of ORD before ER, elements of ER will enter into our ORD discussions. For that reason, I remind you of both awareness and choice in applying the model.

## The Big Picture

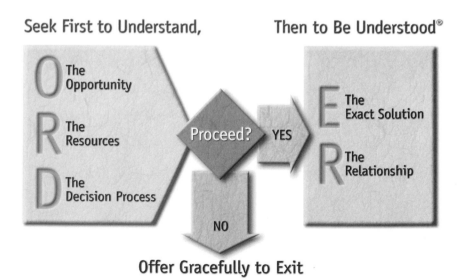

Seek First to Understand, Then to Be Understood®

O — The Opportunity
R — The Resources
D — The Decision Process

Proceed? — YES — NO

E — The Exact Solution
R — The Relationship

Offer Gracefully to Exit

## Opportunity

You can't help someone succeed who has no perceived needs or wants. In the **Opportunity** step, we will mutually develop a sound business case for the proposed solution—or discover that a solution does not exist. We will examine the *issues* the client faces, the *evidence* of their existence, the *impact* of those issues on the organization, the *context* in which those issues exist, and the *constraints* that exist in finding and implementing a solution.

## Resources

Even if there is a substantial opportunity, you can't help someone succeed who has insufficient resources. In the **Resources** step, we will make sure there is congruence between the client's belief and our belief about the *time*, *people*, and *money* necessary and available to achieve the opportunity.

## Decision Process

Even if there is a substantial opportunity with available resources, you can't help someone succeed who can't make a decision. In the **Decision Process**, we will gain mutually clarity on the decision *steps*, the *decisions* to be made, *when* they will decide, *who* is involved in each step, and *how* they will decide. During the process, we will ensure we find out the "how" directly from the "who"—that we develop a solution that exactly meets the client's needs by talking directly to the key owners of the needs.

## Proceed or Exit?

Only if we feel there is a good fit based on our work during ORD, (and we have turned significant yellow lights to green), will we develop and present a solution in ER.

## Exact Solution

In the **Exact Solution** step, we will give evidence and proof that we can help our client resolve their problems and/or achieve their desired results in a way that fits their available resources and matches their decision criteria. With confidence we know we can, or we wouldn't have arrived at this point with our client! Since proposals don't help people succeed (only people do), we will work to make our presentations in person rather than in writing.

## Relationship

In response to our presentation, our client will say yes, no, or no decision. For each of those responses in the **Relationship** step, there are a series of needed actions to ensure a positive and productive ongoing relationship.

## Separate and Equal

We need to do our best possible job on ORD before moving to ER. If it isn't a qualified opportunity with sufficient available resources, and if there isn't a clearly defined decision process with access to the people we need to see, neither our client nor we have earned the solution.

In addition, the competencies, skill sets, and mental models for ORD are different than those for ER. For example:

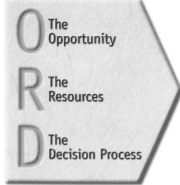

O The Opportunity

R The Resources

D The Decision Process

E The Exact Solution

R The Relationship

- *Divergent thinking:* developing multiple issues, considering many possibilities, talking to many people, systemic thinking

- *Inquiry—seeking* first to understand

- *Understanding effects* of problems

- *Deciding* fit

- *Convergent thinking:* driving to a decision, resolving issues and concerns, implementation, measurement, continuous improvement

- *Advocacy—seeking* to be understood

- *Understanding causes* of problems

- *Executing* and *developing* fit

If you find yourself temporarily lost at any stage of the business development process (or even later in the book), coming back to this chapter should give you your bearings. Before we apply ORDER, there is an important distinction to be made.

ORDER

## The Sales Continuum

Straightforward                 Complex

| Straightforward | Complex |
| --- | --- |
| • Single person | • Many people |
| • Single call | • Multiple calls |
| • Single issue | • Multiple issues |
| • Uncomplicated issues | • Complicated issues |
| • Little money | • Large investment |
| • Lower value-added? | • High value-added? |
| • Price-sensitive? | • Results-sensitive? |
| • Lower margins? | • High margins? |

In applying ORDER to business development, we will work toward the complex end of this spectrum. For straightforward, noncommodity sales, you'll find the ORDER process helpful, and you'll also have to move through it much more quickly and in less depth. For straight commodity or highly transactional sales, this process may need to be modified to serve you well.

# 9
# The Opportunity

Move Off the Solution

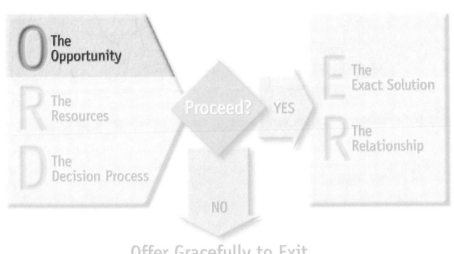

When we meet with a client, we have a checklist that helps us mutually explore the Opportunity:

☐ **Move off the solution.**

☐ Get out all of the issues.

☐ Develop evidence and impact.

☐ Explore context and constraints.

In this chapter, we'll talk about how to "move off the solution" during an opportunity discussion. To go along with that rule, we'll add another: Start anywhere, go everywhere. Then we can talk more intelligently about where you go once you are "off the solution."

## Solutions Have No Inherent Value

Everything the client asks of you, and everything you offer a client, is an intended solution. When you walk in the door and they ask you for something, anything, it's likely to be a request for a solution (We need a…, We want…, We're looking for…, Do you…, Can you help us with…). When you offer them something, it's likely to be a solution. Solutions have no inherent value. Solutions *only* derive value from the problems they solve and/or the results they produce. Understanding this guides everything else we do with clients.

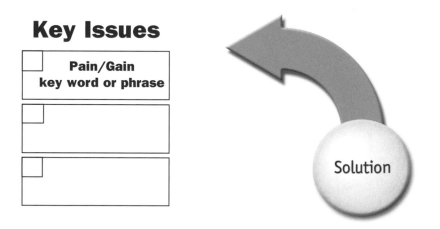

This one paradigm shift has large implications. If it makes sense to you, you will be unable to talk about any of your solutions unless

you've first talked about the problems the solution is supposed to solve and/or the results it's supposed to achieve. Otherwise, it's not a solution, it's an event. It might be an entertaining event, a well-received event, but it's only an event, not a solution. Solutions must actually solve something.

## A Mutual Conspiracy

There's a mutual conspiracy between client and consultant to talk about the solution. We love talking about the solution. It's our comfort zone. We understand it, we know it, it's about us, it's our solution, and it's really great. What about the client? They'd like to think there is a magic bullet—that they can throw some money at the situation and everything will be okay. It's a lot easier talking about a solution than doing the critical spadework to uncover the issues the solution is supposed to resolve, evidence that proves they have a problem, measurements for success, systemic implications, constraints to overcome, etc. And as long as the solution is the topic of discussion, they can put all the pressure on us, sit back, and watch us dance. Because we habitually talk about the solution, to move off the solution will require some discipline and high EQ.

## The Big Marshmallow

In his book *Emotional Intelligence*, Dr. Daniel Goleman, a man who has studied and researched the idea of emotional intelligence, refers to a remarkable study conducted by Walter Mischel during the 1960s at a preschool on Stanford University's campus. I'll give you the quick version of the study. He took children who were about four years old

and put them in a room alone with a big marshmallow on the table. The researcher would tell the child he or she could have the marshmallow, and if the child could wait while the researcher ran a quick errand (15 to 20 minutes), they would bring back two big marshmallows (for a child, a pretty good return on investment!). Then the researcher would leave the room and they would film the child. Some of the kids just couldn't handle it. The idea of waiting to eat that marshmallow was way beyond them, and so they would grab the marshmallow and eat it. Some of them would eat just one small bite, then eat another small bite, and pretty soon the whole marshmallow had disappeared. Some of them would agonize as they walked around the room, staring at it, sniffing it, even licking it, but they wouldn't eat it. Some even tried taking naps. After following up on these children over a long period of time (about 15 years), the kids who had the patience and discipline (impulse resistance) to not eat the marshmallow during the experiment showed characteristics later in life that proved to make them more successful, emotionally and intellectually, regardless of their chosen pursuits.

We find similar results with the best business developers and consultants. If they can resist the impulse to talk about the solution (the adult version of the marshmallow), they get a whole bunch of business with a client rather than just the one obvious opportunity that's in front of them. In other words, they get a bag of marshmallows later instead of one marshmallow at the moment. One of the hardest behaviors to overcome is the tendency to go for the first solution right off the bat. And yet, just like those children, it's been proven that con-

**Opportunity**
Move Off the Solution

sultants who can resist the immediate solution are more successful.
So move off the solution. Don't get trapped into talking about the
solution, because solutions don't make sense unless they're related to
problems they solve or results they produce.

## Where Do You Go When You Move Off the Solution?

The quick answer is anywhere, as long as you go everywhere. I'll
explain that later. To begin, it is certainly appropriate to clarify the solution so you know what it is you are moving off of. For example:

Client:      "Can you help us create a decision support system?"

Consultant:    "It's very likely. Decision support systems (DSS) mean
something different to almost every company. What
exactly were you looking for?"

Even if we clarify the solution, we still have to find either the problems it solves or the results it produces. The client is either strongly
dissatisfied with the current situation, or strongly desirous of results
in the future that won't happen unless something changes. If neither,
we have to question what would motivate them to spend a lot of
money with us.

### Problems

Client:      "Can you help us create a decision support system?"

Consultant:    "That's certainly one of our core competencies. What

kinds of *problems* are you experiencing by not having the right kind of decision support system?"

## Results

Client:      "Can you help us create a decision support system?"

Consultant:  "Well, let's find out. Let's say we put in the world's best decision support system. What *results* would you achieve as a business that you can't get today?"

If we don't know whether to go for problems or results, we can move to the "issues."

## Issues

Client:      "Can you help us create a decision support system?"

Consultant:  "We'd be glad to help. Could you help me understand what *issues* you are trying to address with a decision support system?"

Some behavioral psychologists say that human beings make *all* decisions based on either moving away from pain (something they don't want), or moving toward gain (something they do want). And they also say the motivation to move away from the pain that is immediate is greater than the motivation to move toward the promise of gain in the future. The pain/gain continuum is contextual—people will be motivated differently in different situations. In the same situation, different people will have different motivations.

People who are trying to "move away from pain" will interpret issues as pain, and may give us a list of problems, frustrations, and dissatisfaction. They may even use physical or emotional pain phrases like: "It's killing us…," "We're bleeding…," "It's a pain in the neck…," "It's a real headache…," "It's a nightmare…," "It's like pulling teeth…."

People who are "moving toward gain" will interpret issues as results (i.e., objectives, goals, and outcomes). They may use phrases like: "What we'd like to see…," "What we think is possible…," "Our vision is…," "What we're excited about is…," "Our end in mind is…," "We'd like to create…," etc. Their language will give us some hints about where they would like to start. We'll just need to be aware of the language.

**If we cannot uncover significant pain or gain, then we have a yellow light.**

If we are going to get real, we have to find the motivation driving the solution—the problems it is supposed to solve, the results it is meant to achieve and with which issues. (And please use any synonyms with which you're more comfortable that accomplish the same purpose). *If we cannot uncover significant pain or gain, then we have a yellow light.* In which case we say, "I have a concern!" or "I'm confused!" or "I think we may have a problem!"

## MOVE OFF THE SOLUTION CHALLENGE

Write down 20 "requests for solutions" you commonly hear. For each one write:

- A clarifying question.
- A question moving to a list of problems, challenges, and concerns.
- A question moving to a list of results or outcomes.
- A question moving to a list of issues.

Practice your responses until they are completely natural. The magic is not in what you write; the magic is in the ability to hear a solution and move off to a list of issues the solution is intended to resolve. To avoid premature solutions, you must be made of solution-resistant material. And when you're not sure where to go, remember that you can start anywhere and go everywhere.

# 10
# The Opportunity

Get Out All of the Issues

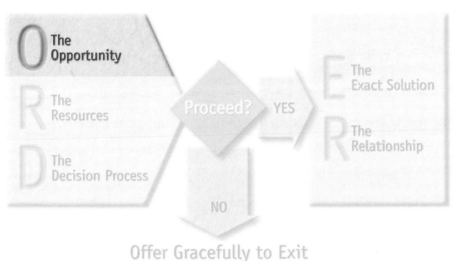

Remember the checklist for mutually exploring the Opportunity:

☑ Move off the solution.

☐ **Get out all of the issues.**

☐ Develop evidence and impact.

☐ Explore context and constraints.

We've talked about moving off the solution. Now let's talk about getting out all of the issues.

## Structure the Conversation

You'll never take a modern sales course where you aren't told to "find out the client's needs." Consultants know they have to ask a few questions before they launch into their pitch. I've heard so many of them begin with a clichéd question like, "So, what's been keeping you up at night?" They then take the first thing the client says, ask a few more questions, and proceed to tell the client how they can help. Or the client starts a 20-minute rambling, disjointed monologue that is extremely hard to capture in a meaningful way. A lot has been said, yet neither consultant nor client takes away a lot of value.

An alternative to the one-sided monologue is to structure the conversation. You can be informal in structuring the conversation and make it completely invisible to the client, or you can explicitly state what you'd like to do to mutually explore the issues. To structure a conversation, you:

- **Get a quick list of all the issues.**
- **Make sure the list is complete.**
- **Find out what matters most.**
- **Go into depth (evidence, impact, context, constraints).**
- **Summarize.**
- **Prioritize (take each issue in order of importance).**

## A "Quick List"

The first thing we would like to get from the client is a "quick list" of all the key issues (problems, results) the solution is meant to address. We want to make sure the list is complete. Our goal is to get out *all* of the issues before talking about any *one* issue. Real-life dialogue makes this a challenging goal, yet it is our goal nonetheless.

When we ask a client something like "What specific business issues are you hoping this solution will address?" it is not uncommon for them to give us one or two issues off the top of their head. It is also very common for consultants to immediately go into depth on those issues. Rather than jumping into the first few issues that surface, practice patience and discipline to ask, "What else?" Then you will have a *complete* list of issues before going into depth on any *one* issue. When you get the full list, and then ask which is most important, the client often selects as the most important issue one that is toward or at the end of the list. They will sometimes pick an item that they only added to the list when you invited them to make sure the list was complete.

If you immediately explore the first one or two issues instead of getting a complete list, you risk the following:
1. You will never get the complete list (and may miss significant opportunities).
2. You will end up talking about *an* issue, which is not *the* most important issue.

3. Even if you eventually discover the most important issue, you may have depleted the scarce resources of time and energy.

## Sound Bites of Pain and Gain

Successfully getting a complete list of the issues will require you to listen carefully to what people are telling you, and capture the issue in a key word or phrase that describes a problem (pain) or result (gain). The issue, ideally, should be *in their words.* If their solution were the title of a book (*Customer Relationship Management at General Express*), the key words or phrases they use would be the chapter headings. Sometimes the client will speak in chapter headings. Sometimes we have to listen to the client read the entire chapter before we can assign the heading. One way or the other, we want to end up with a complete list of issues.

Let's say the client asks for project management software (a solution). We might clarify what they mean by project management software. We will then move them off the solution to the issues project management software is meant to address.

The client might begin by describing what has been going on over the last five years, both with the company and in the industry, and conclude by saying they have downsized from 20,000 employees to 10,000. Is downsizing a problem or a result for this client? Neither! It is simply a fact. To explore downsizing further we might say, "And what did downsizing cause?" If they were to say, "Well, we have to do more with fewer people, and that's putting real pressure on everyone,"

then we might say, "And are you hoping project management software will help?" If their answer is yes, we now have one issue, one sound bite, one chapter heading: "Downsizing—need more from less."

At this point, we continue to get a list of the issues and avoid the temptation to go into more detail. "That's helpful. At a high level, what else are you hoping project management software will address?" With patience, discipline, and skill, let's say we get the following list:

- Downsizing—need more from less
- Missed deadlines
- Unhappy customers
- Increased costs
- Low morale

If the client says, "That about covers it," we check to make sure the list is complete. "Take a look at the list. If you could make major progress against these goals, *and nothing else*, would you have a solution that exactly met your needs?" Maybe after pondering, the client says, "Well, we also need to improve time to market, and good project management should make a big contribution to that." We add "Improve time to market" to our list.

| Downsizing—Need More From Less |
| Missed Deadlines |
| Unhappy Customers |
| Increased Costs |
| Low Morale |
| Improve Time to Market |

Solution

## Adding to the List

So far, we are just getting their list. When they are finished, and feel there is nothing more they can add, as experts we may feel the list is missing some issues. Because we are committed to no guessing, we test out our hypothesis by asking, "I noticed you didn't mention improved quality. Is that at all an issue for you?" We've invited the client to either say it is an issue and add it to the list, or to say it's not an issue and leave it off for the time being. They may also say they included that as part of another issue, and we are now aware it's rolled up into another phrase or word. When we're finished with this step, we should arrive at a complete list of the issues mutually.

## What Matters Most?

Once we've arrived at a complete list, we can now prioritize the issues. We can say, "I'm sure all of these issues are important and interrelated. Is there one you feel has the most leverage or impact?" The client often picks one, and you can now go into depth on evidence and impact. If the client has trouble identifying only one and says they are all important or picks multiple issues, you have a couple of choices:

1. Say, "They *are* all important. I'll make sure we discuss them all. Which one would you like to talk about first?" The client will self-select priority.

2. Take the multiple issues as one issue, and move on to developing evidence and impact.

## What About Groups?

If you are working with a group of people, you can get a prioritized list of issues using a facilitation technique called "N/3." Get the group to brainstorm a complete list of issues (no discussion, no debate, no right or wrong, no good or bad—just a complete list). Number them on a flip chart. Take the total number of issues and divide by 3. Give each participant that number (N/3) of votes. For example, if there are 21 issues, each person gets 7 votes. Have them vote for N issues. Then poll the group to see how many voted for each issue. Some facilitators allow individuals to place multiple votes on a single issue; some make them place each vote on a unique issue. In a short amount of time you can have a prioritized list of issues for the group.

## Tools, Not Rules

Structuring the conversation is a tool. The tool should serve you, not you serve the tool. However you accomplish it, the ability to get out all of the issues and tackle them in some priority will add immediate value to both the client and you.

**If we can not uncover significant pain or gain, then we have a yellow light.**

**GET OUT THE ISSUES CHALLENGE**

In your next several client conversations, see how well you can get out all of the issues before going into depth on any one issue.

**Opportunity**
Get Out All of the Issues

# 11
# The Opportunity

Evidence

Again, our Opportunity checklist is:

☑ Move off the solution.

☑ Get out all of the issues.

☐ **Develop evidence** and impact.

☐ Explore context and constraints.

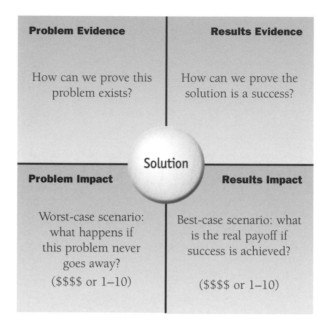

| Problem Evidence | Results Evidence |
|---|---|
| How can we prove this problem exists? | How can we prove the solution is a success? |

Solution

| Problem Impact | Results Impact |
|---|---|
| Worst-case scenario: what happens if this problem never goes away?<br>($$$$ or 1–10) | Best-case scenario: what is the real payoff if success is achieved?<br>($$$$ or 1–10) |

We have now moved off the solution, and we have a complete list of issues. Of that complete list, each issue is a problem to be solved or a result to be produced. Problems and results can be further developed by two key components: *evidence* of their existence, and their *impact* on the organization.

## In God We Trust, All Others...

As I walk out of my office, there is a sign on a colleague's desk that says, "In God we trust. All others bring data." This is the attitude we bring to evidence. For a problem, how do we know it's a problem? What is there too much or too little of? By how much? Do they have *too little* profits, *too limited* revenue, *too many* complaints, *too many* rejects? For a result, how will we measure success? What must increase or decrease? By how much? If we don't understand which numbers are too small or too big, it will be hard (if not close to

impossible) to understand which numbers our solution is supposed
to increase or decrease.

If a client says they have a problem with quality, what's letting them
know it's a problem? How do they *measure* quality? What are those
measures *now*? What *should* they be? If they say they want improved
customer satisfaction, how do they measure customer satisfaction?
What are those measures now? What would the client like them to
be? Is somebody looking at a report, seeing a number they don't like,
and attributing it to this requested solution? The bottom line is,
"Show me the data!"

If they have data of where they are now, what's telling them that's a
problem? What's giving rise to the belief that the number should be
*different*? If they want a number in the future, what's letting them
know that's the *right* number? What's leading them to believe the
number is *realistic*? Where are they in relationship to that number
today? If they want us, as experts, to suggest what the number should
be, how will we back up our claims?

## Opportunity or Vulnerability?

The lack of evidence (problem, result, or both) is either an opportunity or a vulnerability. How could it be an opportunity? If there is no
evidence of the problem, we can help them get it. We can facilitate a
diagnostic. By diagnosing, they get a chance to spend a little bit of
time and money defining the problem before they spend a lot of time
and money trying to fix it. They also get a low-risk exposure to what

it's like to work with us, and we with them. And the diagnostic will either prove or disprove the need for the larger solution.

What if they have no way to measure the results of the solution? If measuring results is important, we can help them develop a measurement system. Then we both get an opportunity to prove the solution worked.

How are we vulnerable if there is no evidence? First, *solution approval is vulnerable.* Someone, somewhere in the organization may say, "Before we spend large sums of money with these people, could someone please prove to me that we have a problem?" Or he or she might say, "Before we write a check for this, could someone please tell me how we will know it's money well spent?" Without evidence, people in the client's organization can shoot down the proposed solution for lack of sound, critical thought or a good business case, and perhaps rightly so. It may also allow competing (and possibly less important) priorities to ascend, based on more accurate and complete analysis or better promotion.

Second, *solution execution is vulnerable.* How do we know we are solving the *right* problem? How do we even know it *is* a problem? How will we prevent "scope creep"? How will we know when we are finished? How will we know if we are *successful*? Remember our rule of no guessing. Without evidence, we are forced to guess.

## A Lexicon of Evidence

To avoid guessing, there is a process for uncovering the evidence. The key words for finding evidence are:

> How, What, Where, Which, Who, When
> …Specifically

For example, evidence questions for a problem might include:

- How do you know it's a problem?
- What lets you know there is a problem?
- Where specifically does the problem show up?
- Which measures prove there is a problem?
- Who specifically is most affected by the problem?
- When does this problem most often occur?

For a result, we add the future-tense words "would" or "will":

- How specifically would you measure success?
- What would let you know we were successful?
- Where would the success of this project show up?
- Which performance indicators will increase or decrease if we are successful?
- Who specifically would be most affected by these issues?
- When do you need these results in place?

### EVIDENCE CHALLENGE 1

Make a list of typical issues you hear from clients. Then list problem-evidence or results-evidence questions you could ask.

## Types of Evidence

In asking these questions, we are looking for particular types of evidence. There are four types of evidence likely to be found:

1. **No evidence.** They have no evidence that substantiates either the existence of a problem or accomplishment of a result.

2. **Soft evidence.** They have anecdotal evidence (word of mouth, statistically insignificant surveys).

3. **Presumed evidence.** They have data from third-party sources such as research groups, consulting firms, publications, or industry associations. This evidence applies to groups or categories, and may or may not apply to the client's organization.

4. **Hard evidence.** They have data within the organization that proves there is a problem, or metrics for measuring the accomplishment of a result.

Of all four types of evidence, clearly we are pushing ourselves—and the client—for hard evidence.

## A Predictable Path

Either they have it,   or they don't have it.

When we ask the client for evidence, *either they have it or they don't.* (Even I was able to figure that one out.) It is surprising to find that even when we are talking to people intimately connected to the issues, they often can't come up with evidence, or the evidence is soft. It is less surprising when we are talking to people at organizational levels removed from the problems or results. Lack of evidence is common when someone has been delegated to "go get some information"

about a solution. Lack of evidence is common when we talk to specialists (like IT or HR people) about evidence for business issues. It is common with committees or task forces. It is common, period. Then why isn't it more common for consultants to insist on diagnostics before proceeding to solutions? I wish diagnostics were more common.

When the client does not have evidence, *either someone else does or nobody does.* (I'm on a roll.) If someone else does, the logical questions are "Who?" and "When can we talk to them?" This is an opportunity to move from people who don't know to people who do.

Somebody else has it,
- Who?
- When can we talk to them?

or nobody has it.
- Is it important?
- Would you like some help?

If *nobody* has the evidence, my question is, *"Is it important?"* Is it important to get this evidence in order to build a good business case for the solution? If it is not important to the people we are talking to (perhaps they live with it everyday and don't need data to know it's a problem), we need to know if it is important to someone who has to allocate funds and will only do so if there is a good business case.

If it is important to get the evidence, *can they get it themselves or do they need some help?* Often they will say they need some help. At this point, they have sold themselves on a diagnostic. Eighty percent of the time, when information is important and they haven't been able to get it on their own, they will want some help.

And what about the 20 percent of the time where they say they will get the evidence themselves? If it's critical information, and they've

never been able to get it on their own, what are the reasons they don't have it? With the intent to help them succeed, we can push on that idea a little bit. Typically what I say is, "Well, great. If you can, that's excellent. Just out of curiosity—and please don't take this personally—if it's such important data, and you've never been able to get it before, what's going to change tomorrow?" Frequently I hear, "Probably nothing. I guess we do need some help." The 20 percent has just dropped to 10 percent. And to the 10 percent I'm going to say, "Great. Let's set some deadlines and agree ahead of time that if you can't meet those deadlines, and it's still important, you'll bring us in and we'll do it." I can live with 10 percent in those circumstances.

### EVIDENCE CHALLENGE 2

Look over your last three projects or proposals. How tight was your evidence—both current-state (problem) and future-state (results)? Look at any outstanding proposals and ask the question, "What could I do to improve evidence for these scenarios?" In your next few conversations, concentrate on asking better evidence questions and whether a diagnostic makes sense.

In the next chapter, we will examine how to turn the evidence they have into an impact on their organization.

# 12
# The Opportunity

Impact—Hard Measures

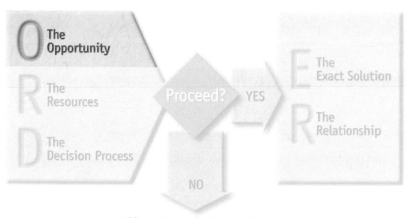

Just to keep track of where we are, our Opportunity checklist is:

- ☑ Move off the solution.
- ☑ Get out all of the issues.
- ☐ **Develop** evidence and **impact**.
- ☐ Explore context and constraints.

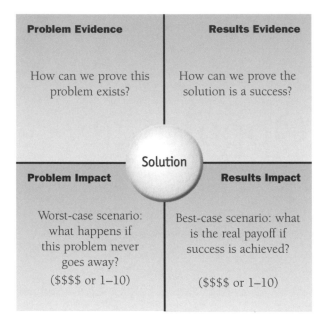

## So What and Who Cares?

If *problem evidence* is "How do we know it's a problem?" then *problem impact* is "How big or how bad is the problem?" What is it costing the organization to have this problem? If the problem is never fixed (worst-case scenario), what happens?

If *result evidence* is "How will we measure success?" then *result impact* is "How big or how beneficial is the payoff?" What is the return on investment, short and long term, direct and opportunity, tangible and intangible? If everything goes right (best-case scenario), what do we win? Impact answers the question "So what and who cares?" Our EQ awareness might suggest we ask those questions with a little more tact; nonetheless, that is what we want to know.

## Moving From Evidence to Impact

When the client actually has some evidence (hard, soft, or presumed), we turn the evidence into impact. Let's look at how we would turn each type of evidence into impact. If the client has an issue that can be directly measured (hard), we ask five questions:

1. **How do you measure it?**
2. **What is it now?** (current-state evidence)
3. **What would you like it to be?** (future-state evidence)
4. **What's the value of the difference?** (impact)
5. **What's the value of the difference over time?** (impact over the appropriate management horizon)

For instance:

Client: "Having this information would increase our productivity."

Us: "How do you measure productivity?"

Client: "Widgets per hour."

Us: "How many widgets do you produce per hour now?"

Client: "One thousand."

Us: "Let's say you had the information you wanted. How many do you think you could produce with that information?"

Client: "Closer to 1,500."

Us: "If you could increase your widget production by 50 percent, what would that do to revenues (or margins, contribution, profits, etc.)?"

Client: "Well, we do $100 million in widgets now. If we could sell all the increased production, that would be $50 million."

Us:  "So without growing or compounding, over the next two to three years that would be an additional $100 million to $150 million?"

This example is simplistic, but you get the idea. And when the value of the difference is immediately apparent in dollars, you can drop out Questions 1 and 4. For example:

Client:  "Not having account management software is hurting sales."

Us:  (2) "What are sales now?"

Client:  "$500 million."

Us:  (3) "Let's say you had account management software that was really doing the job. What would you expect sales to be then?"

Client:  "$550 million."

Us:  (5) "So over the next three to five years you'd be looking at revenue growth of $150 million to $250 million?"

The real art form is quantifying the impact when the value of the difference is not immediately apparent in dollars. For instance, if the client believes the key issue is quality:

Us:  (1) "How do you measure quality?"

Client:  "Number of rejections per thousand units."

Us:  (2) "What is the current rejection rate?"

Client:  "Ten per thousand units."

Us:  (3) "Let's say we were successful with this TQM project. What would you expect it to be?"

Client:     "Five per thousand units."

Us:          (4) "What's the value of the difference?"

Well…a lot, a considerable amount, big bucks! And that's the problem. We have just asked the client to do a lot of math in his or her
head. If you want to mutually discover the impact (so the client also
has a sense of the impact), do some "back of the envelope" math to
work with the client to come up the amount. Here are two
approaches:

## Chunking It Down

Us:          "Roughly (ballpark), what does it cost for one rejection?"

Client:     "$1,000."

Us:          "So that's $5,000 you would save per 1,000 units pro-
             duced. How many units do you produce annually?"

Client:     "Three million total."

Us:          "So 3,000,000 divided by 1,000 is 3,000. Three thousand
             times $5,000 is $15 million. Does that sound right?"

Client:     "Yeah, that's very close."

Us:          "So over two to three years you are looking at somewhere
             between $30 million to $45 million wrapped up in this
             quality issue?"

In chunking it down, we've allowed the client to go through the
process with us so he or she understands the impact of the numbers
as well as we do, and that the numbers are legitimate.

## Rolling It Up

Us:     "What do you spend on rejections each year—roughly, ballpark?"

Client:     "Tens of millions."

Us:     "Closer to two or three, or closer to eight or nine?"

Client:     "About $25 million to $30 million."

Us:     "So if you cut that in half you would save around $12.5 million to $15 million a year?"

Client:     "Yeah."

Us:     "So over two to three years, you are looking at somewhere between $25 million to $45 million wrapped up in this quality issue?"

## "Back of the Envelope" Economics

Some people are insecure about doing "back of the envelope" math or economics. We're not running complex spreadsheets and pretending this is a hard-core financial analysis. We're grabbing the nearest notepad or scrap paper and jotting down some preliminary numbers. Here is an example of hard-core financial analysis. Let's say you have three proposed projects (three of anything really), and you have to figure out which one you're supposed to do for the best return on investment. First you project the revenue out five to ten years in the future (what a guess!). Then project the costs out five to ten years in the future (Guess #2). Really hard, precise numbers so far, right? Then subtract the costs from the revenue and you have profits. Divide those profits by the average weighted cost of capital (which is another

guess—nobody knows what that really is). So you have a stream of guesses about revenue, you subtract another stream of guesses about costs, and you divide that by a guess about the weighted cost of capital, and you come up with net present value. You then look at the three net present values (guesses), and the one with the highest number is the one you're supposed to pick.

If you don't like the one you're supposed to pick, what do you do? You go back and change all of your guesses until they say what you want or expect. And that's what we call hard-core financial analysis. Nobody is pretending these guesses are reality. *The purpose of the exercise is to take guesses and opinions about the future, and talk about them in the common denominator of money.* By doing so, business people can communicate more effectively about their opinions, share and test their assumptions, and hopefully make better decisions—or at least more educated guesses.

What we're doing isn't much different. We are just asking people to talk about complex issues in the common language of money. Remember, you will offer your solution in currency. If the client can't put some financial return to the cost of the problem(s) or the value of the result(s), then your solution is naked. They will be measuring diverse opinions against hard currency. We have not helped them make a good decision in their own best interest. So please, get comfortable—and skillful—with "back of the envelope" economics. Clothe your solutions with the impact of money.

> **Take guesses and opinions about the future, and talk about them in the common denominator of money.**

## Helpful Hints

When doing "back of the envelope" economics, use words and phrases like "ballpark," "rough estimate," "more or less," "best guess," "finger to the wind." We want to know if we are talking tens of thousands, hundreds of thousands, millions, tens of millions, hundreds of millions…order of magnitude. The size of the solution should be at least somewhat commensurate to the size of the problem. We need some sense of how big an opportunity this is so we can give our client some sense of what they should do about it. Turn all non-dollar figures into dollars. Don't end up with percentages or ratios without explicitly converting them to money.

Have the client run the numbers with you or for you. Don't sit there with your financial calculator and spend five minutes punching buttons then announce, "Wow, you have a $20 million problem!" At that point, *they* don't have a $20 million problem, even if your numbers are right. *You and your financial calculator* have a $20 million problem! Work on the problem with them, not for them. They need a sense of ownership in this from the beginning. Don't start excluding them when you're trying to determine financial impact.

If the numbers come up big, don't gloat or give out the vibration of "Gotcha!" Be the conservative one. Say something like, "That seems like a large number. Is that realistic?" That gives them a chance to either modify it to come up with a number they believe in, or to say something like, "Well, if anything, it's probably underestimated."

Remember that the goal is not to "get them"—the goal is to get real.

And finally, remember, it's not a problem until they say it's a problem. I've had clients who quickly calculated a $20 million cost to an issue, and didn't see it as a problem. If they are a $40 billion company the $20 million might not be important relative to other priorities. Of course, if that is the case, we'd like to get a "quick list" of those other priorities.

## The Measurable Alert

Every company has measurables. They all have some form of financial measures, operational measures, performance measures, technology or process measures, customer satisfaction measures, etc. I'm not saying they are the right measures nor am I saying they are accurate. I'm just saying they have them. What is heartbreaking is to listen to a consultant interview a client, have the client sprinkle the conversation with measurables, and watch the consultant not follow up on even one. To be at the top of our profession, we need to have finely tuned measurable alerts within our nervous system. When we hear (or offer) something we can measure that is directly related to the issues the solution is supposed to resolve, our measurable alert should fire off and we can ask five questions (or whatever will accomplish the same outcome):

1. How do you measure it?
2. What is it now? (current-state evidence)
3. What would you like it to be? (future-state evidence)

4. What's the value of the difference? (impact)

5. What's the value of the difference over time? (impact over the appropriate management horizon)

### IMPACT CHALLENGE

In your next several interviews, increase your attention to the measurables the client offers. Ask for some if none are offered. See how well you can turn hard measures into impact. See if you can develop some "back of the envelope" economics either for the cost of the problems, or for the value of the results.

# 13
# The Opportunity

Impact—Soft Measures

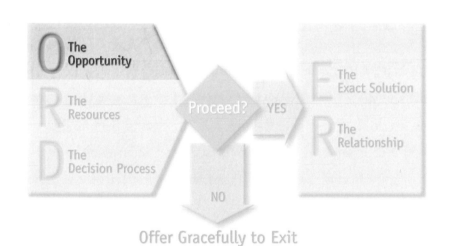

We are still talking about the Opportunity and impact.

☑ Move off the solution.

☑ Get out all of the issues.

☐ **Develop** evidence and **impact**.

☐ Explore context and constraints.

## Soft Measures

So far we've been quantifying the impact of when the client offers us (or we offer them) something we can measure (hard evidence). They often give us issues that are hard to quantify. They may say they want to improve communication, enhance competitive position, or have better relations with clients. Maybe they say they have a problem with morale, trust, or motivation. Perhaps they don't feel they are getting the most out of their people, their marketing, or their reputation in the marketplace. They need a strategic approach, a better plan, creative thinking, more innovation, improved teamwork, or visionary leadership. How will we and the client quantify the value of these issues?

## Peeling the Onion

To quantify the value of the issues, we will need to get to the heart of the matter. To do that, we "peel the onion." Our goal in peeling the onion is to move from a broad, generic description of an issue to the underlying motivation or key driver. From an IQ perspective, we move from soft measures to hard. From an EQ perspective, we move from that which is known, intellectual, and safe, to that which is unexamined, emotional, and possibly vulnerable. We are trying to get real about what makes this important—intellectually and emotionally.

If we start with a problem—something the client wants to remove, avoid, or move away from—then we will "peel for pain." If we start with a result—something they want to achieve, obtain, or move toward—we will "peel for gain."

The key discrimination we need to make in peeling the onion is the difference between going *around* a level of investigation, and going *down* a level of investigation. We will recognize going around levels as evidence, and going down levels as impact. Most consultants get lost in going around (collecting evidence), and either are unwilling or unable to go down and strip away enough layers to get to the true impact, to the heart of the matter. The best way to describe peeling the onion is to give some examples.

Questions that go "around" a level of inquiry.

Questions that go "down" a level of inquiry.

## Peeling for Gain

The key phrase when peeling for gain is, "What would that allow you to do?" To peel for gain, listen to what the client says they want. Key phrases you'll hear that cue you to peel for gain include:

- "Our goal is to…"
- "The objectives we are striving for are…"
- "We are looking to accomplish…"
- "Our targets in the future are…"
- "In the ideal world…"
- "The improvements we're looking for are…"

While you may pause to ask some evidence questions along the way, your focus is to give the client what they said they wanted and then ask, "What does that allow you to do that you can't do today?" We can certainly vary how we ask that question: "What does that get you?" "Where do the benefits of that show up?" "How does that impact performance?" "How does that help the bottom line?" "Best-case scenario, what will be the ultimate gain?" and so on. The key is to keep stripping away layers until we get to something that is a key business driver (ideally, a hard measure), a key emotional driver, or both.

For example, if the client says, "What we really need here is improved communication," we would peel down and say, "And if you improved your communication, what would that allow you to do that you can't do today?" The client might then answer, "We would get the right information to the right people at the right time." At this level, we would peel down and say, "And if you could get the right information to the right people at the right time, what would that allow you to do?" "We would make better business decisions."

Peel to the next layer—"And if you could make better business decisions, what would that allow you to do?"—you might hear, "We would increase revenues, profits, bonuses, stock prices, and customer satisfaction." At this point, we have gotten to something we can measure, and we can ask five questions:

1. How do you measure it?
2. What is it now? (current-state evidence)
3. What would you like it to be? (future-state evidence)

4. What's the value of the difference? (impact)

5. What's the value of the difference over time? (impact over the appropriate management horizon)

## Peeling for Pain

Many times we're working with people who are hoping to eliminate pain. They're telling us what they don't want or where it hurts. They may even use words of physical or emotional pain:

- "It's killing us…"
- "We're bleeding…"
- "We have to correct…"
- "It is so painful when…"
- "What's hurting us is…"
- "What's stopping us is…"
- "We are suffering from…"
- "We're concerned about…"

Some consultants find it harder, more uncomfortable, to peel for pain. To them, talking about the wonderful things people want is easier than delving in to the depths of what people don't want. Since clients are often motivated to move away from pain rather than move toward gain, we still need to get to the core motivation. So here is how we peel down for pain. The key phrase is "And then what happens?" Let's look at the following example. The clients says, "Our people have low morale." We say, "And when you have low morale, then what happens?"

When the client answers, "People aren't motivated," we may peel down and ask, "And when people aren't motivated, then what happens?"

Again, we can vary that phrase in many ways: "And what does that affect?" "And what are the consequences of that?" "And what does that in turn impact?" "And how does that hit the bottom line?" "Worst-case scenario, if you never change this, what will happen?"

If the client continues and responds, "When people aren't motivated, they don't align themselves with the business objectives of the company." We continue to peel for pain by saying, "And when they aren't aligned with the business objectives of the company, then what happens?" Once again, when we arrive at a place where we can measure, we can ask:

1. How do you measure it?
2. What is it now? (current-state evidence)
3. What would you like it to be? (future-state evidence)
4. What's the value of the difference? (impact)
5. What's the value of the difference over time? (impact over the appropriate management horizon)

## If You Feel It, Ask It

When doing field research, I often observe that consultants who have been trained in peeling the onion get close to the last level of questioning, and just before they get to the real impact or a

measurable, they bail out to someplace safe like, "How many employees do you have?" and "What's your current version of the software?" Afterwards, when debriefing them, I ask them if they could hear in their mind what the next question should have been. They usually say, "Yes, but clearly the other person would have felt uncomfortable had I asked that question." So being researchers, we go back and ask the client, "If they had asked this question, what would have been your reaction?" They often say, "Tough question...a good question though. I would have liked to talk about that." So often the reason we give for not getting to the heart of the matter is that they would feel uncomfortable. The real reason seems to be that *we* would feel uncomfortable. The irony is that we wait to establish rapport before asking the hard question, yet asking the question can help us establish rapport.

The challenge with evidence questions, although vital, is that people get lost in them because they feel safe there. They forget at some point they're going to have to go down into the impact. And it's not as if clients know their eventual response and they're just waiting for you to peel down so they can tell you. Often they haven't been through the intellectual or emotional rigor to figure out what the real consequence of their problem or opportunity is either. Getting to the heart of the matter provides added value to the client, not just more information to us.

Remember our commitment to no guessing. If neither of us understands the true motivations—the difference that will make a difference—then it

will be difficult to get a solution that exactly meets the client's needs. If we're guessing, exactly which needs are we going to meet?

## If You Can't Quantify, Qualify

Clearly, we are putting an emphasis on quantifying problems and results. Since our solution is in currency, it is helpful for the issues it addresses to be at least roughly described in currency as well. Quantifying helps clients make better decisions. It makes it easier to defend their opinions to others in the organization.

**If you can't quantify, at least strongly qualify.**

Sometimes it is difficult or inappropriate to quantify the impact of an issue. Some business visionaries are successful because they follow their intuition—their dream—and refuse to get bogged down in the analysis. They cut through "paralysis by analysis" and just make things happen. They may not need to quantify the size of a problem to know that it is mission-critical to correct it. They will do whatever it takes. If we are talking to the sole decision maker—a person who does not need to justify his or her decision, and who has sole discretionary power over the budget—we may not need to quantify the problems or results.

In other situations, clients may not have the patience, discipline, trust, or willingness to quantify the impact. Our rule then is, *"If you can't quantify, at least strongly qualify."* One way to qualify is on a scale of 1 to 10. In this way, we are still putting a numeric qualifier on a feeling or belief. This gives both of us more accuracy about the

importance and/or urgency of that belief, and greater facility in comparing it to what others believe.

A sample form of the question is, "On a scale of 1 to 10 (with 10 being mission-critical, you have to do it; and 1 being that it's irritating, but you can live with it), where are you?"

For instance, if the client says, "Well I can't relate morale to productivity; that's too big of a stretch, there are too many other things impacting it," we might say, "That makes sense to me. I can well understand it would be hard to establish a causal link. So give me a sense, on a scale of 1 to 10 (10 being this is mission-critical; and 1 being it's irritating, but who cares), where do you see yourself on that scale?"

If they say they are an 8, a 9, or a 10, what are they saying about their sense of the impact? Pretty urgent. If they say they are about a 5, what are they telling you? It's not that big of a deal. The real questions we're trying to ask is how do they know it's a problem (evidence) and how bad is the problem (impact). If we can't get it into the language of dollars and return on investment (and that's the best thing), at least we can get it on a scale of 1 to 10. We're getting them to commit to a sense of urgency, and if they tell us it's not urgent, we're going to take away the solution. If they say it's a 5, then we have a concern. As much as it may sound like an interesting or exciting project, is it really likely that a company is going to spend their money on a 5 when they could be spending the same money on an 8, a 9, or a 10?

**IMPACT CHALLENGE 1**

In your next several client discussions, listen for soft issues and measures, and peel the onion. If you can't quantify, at least qualify on a scale of 1 to 10. Try it.

## Presumed Measures

I said earlier that evidence can be hard, soft, or presumed. Presumed evidence comes from third parties—research firms, consulting companies, industry associations, publications, major vendors, etc. Often, we can't be completely confident in the source or the accuracy of the information. It's a place to start. If companies have data about their current state, they can use "best practices" data to sense where they could be or what they would have to do to leap-frog the competition. If they have no data, presumed evidence can allow them to say where they *believe* they are, more or less, through a benchmark. (It is worth it to eventually find out the real facts.) Using presumed evidence can also be risky since we can't be sure if we should apply the findings to a particular company; and it may be better than nothing. And if there is a gap between where the client thinks they are and where they think they could be, we can quantify the gap.

For example, we may read a research study that shows 30 percent of all retail business will be done over the Internet by the year 2010, and that those who can lead the way will gain significant competitive advantage. We may ask our client, "Do you think that is likely for your company? If so, what would be the implications?"

## IMPACT CHALLENGE 2

For the predictable issues of your clients, what presumed evidence
could you bring to the table?

# 14
# The Opportunity

## Context

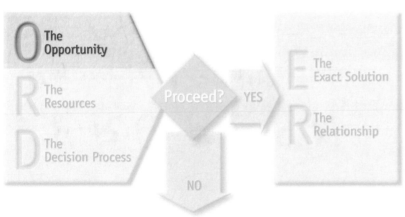

Did it seem like we'd never finish with impact? Actually, as we explore context, we may broaden and deepen our evaluation of the impact. Let's remember where we are:

☑ Move off the solution.

☑ Get out all of the issues.

☑ Develop evidence and impact.

☐ **Explore context** and constraints.

There are two elements of context we will discuss:

1. **Operational context.** Who or what else does this issue (or these issues) affect?
2. **Organizational context.** How does this solution fit into the big picture?

## The Organizational Ecosystem

When working with clients, we are often looking at one part of an organization. That part exists in a system. Rarely do solutions exist in isolation. We, as consultants, need to be aware of the interconnections of the client's ecosystem and look closely at the impact of the changes our solution will make. If we are going to change one part of the system, we should know who or what else is affected by our solution. The basic tenets of systems thinking have been popularized by Peter Senge in his book *The Fifth Discipline*, and examined with rigor by numerous authors. My goal here is not to review them; it is to encourage both myself and others to learn and apply them to our work with clients. The more we think systemically, the more likely we will have a solution that truly works for the whole and is sustainable over time.

Many of my clients tell me they want to do more "cross-selling" (what a strange term), that is, introduce many products and services to a client other than the one under current consideration. If we truly believe that those products and services will help the client succeed with perceived problems or results, the introduction is congruent with our intent.

**Opportunity**
Context

When we "get out all of the issues," we may find multiple opportunities to help the client. Some we may be able to help with the products and services of our company. For others, we can make the client aware of our strategic partners in whom we have confidence. For yet others, we may have to acknowledge we can't help. Another opportunity for expanded assistance comes when we ask, "Who or what else do these issues affect?" As we broaden and deepen the mutual understanding of the task at hand, we open the potential for added value.

## Operational Context

The key question we are trying to answer here is "Who or what else is affected by this issue (these issues)?" For instance, we might ask, "Does this affect just you and your department, or does it affect other departments as well?" or, "Does this just affect this process, or does it impact other processes as well?"

**Operational context: Who or what else is affected?**

The focus of this book to this point has been to articulate the results. To this end we have examined *issues, evidence, impact, and context.* When all is said and done, the behaviors and competencies of human beings produce those results. Although they may use technology and benefit by processes, humans are still responsible for the results. Companies attempt to use predictable systems and tools to guide behaviors in a way they believe will produce the results.

One of the tools Franklin Covey uses to help think systemically is the *Organizational Effectiveness Cycle™ (OE Cycle)*. The OE Cycle helps get the systems and tools right. These include what are called, the *Six Rights:*

1. The Right *Processes*
2. The Right *Structure*
3. The Right *People*
4. The Right *Information*
5. The Right *Decisions*
6. The Right *Rewards*

The Six Rights are put in place to achieve the major strategy of the organization, which should serve the ultimate economic and service missions of the organization. All of this is designed to meet the needs of the various stakeholders of the company.

# OE Cycle™

If we were doing "sales training," for instance, we would work first to mutually understand the key business results the client wants to achieve (problems, results). We would then do a diagnostic to determine the current level of competencies available to meet those needs and the opportunities to increase or add ability. We would want to measure competencies before and after our intervention, and even estimate the impact of improvement on the desired results.

We and the client must rigorously ask ourselves the following: Even if we are assured that the training increased competencies as expected, will those results be sustained over time if no changes are made to our other systems and processes? If we don't reward people to perform these competencies, will we improve? If we don't give them the right information to execute and monitor performance, will we succeed? If we don't allow them to make the appropriate decisions, will having access to the right information even matter? If we don't examine how we structure territories, working relationships, and interactions with other parts of the company, will it be sustainable? If we don't increase other competencies and knowledge apart from business development skills, is it likely we will achieve the full potential of the desired results?

These are not the only questions we must answer; they are a start. The question that will guide us is "Who or what else do these issues affect?"

**Opportunity**
Context

**Organizational context:**

**How does this solution fit**

**the "big picture"?**

## Organizational Context—The Big Picture

Looking at the OE Cycle diagram, we'd also like to know how our solution is linked to the mission, vision, and key strategies of the organization. What is going on in the company that affects *every* decision made, not just the one being discussed? I know this is not something that has never occurred to you. I know it's not rocket science. Yet, it continues to astound me (particularly with the information now available on the Internet) how many consultants fail to take time to understand the organizational context of the companies with whom they work. Every company has an explicit or implicit mission. They have values. They have key initiatives or strategies they think will make the company successful. What are they and how do they relate to our solution? Projects that align with organizational context make more sense to more people and are less price-sensitive. To the degree our solutions help meet companywide goals, it will help many people and efforts, not just a few.

### CONTEXT CHALLENGE

For each of your pending solutions, work with the client to find out "Who or what else do these issues affect?" For each of your upcoming interviews, do your homework on the organizational context of your prospective client.

# 15
# The Opportunity

Constraints

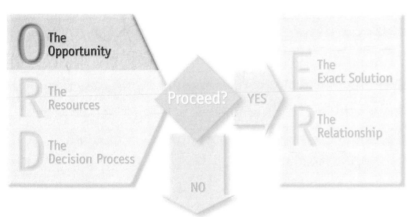

☑ Move off the solution.

☑ Get out all of the issues.

☑ Develop evidence and impact.

☐ **Explore** context and **constraints**.

As I mentioned before, after discussing the issues, evidence, impact, and context, we and our clients should be able to come to one of the following conclusions:

- The impact seems big.
- The impact seems small.
- The impact is not agreed upon (and usually we think it is bigger than they do).

In this and the following chapter, let's examine some sensible actions for each of these scenarios.

## When the Impact Seems Big

We have been exploring the *issues, evidence, impact,* and *context* with the client. If we mutually arrive at the conclusion that the impact is substantial, a fair question arises: If the value of solving the problems and/or producing the results is so worthwhile, what has stopped the client from just making it happen? What have they tried before and what stopped it from working? That may sound counterintuitive; remember, we're trying to get them a solution that exactly meets their needs. If something has stopped it in the past, it's likely to stop it again, and we'll both better off removing the constraints.

## The Constraints Question

If the situation has been going on for a while, the constraints question is, "What has stopped the organization from successfully resolving these issues before now?"

If this is a new opportunity with no history, the constraints question

is, "What, if anything, might prevent the successful implementation of this solution from going forward?"

The answer to this question can provide valuable insight. For whatever reason, it is not often asked. Perhaps consultants fear, at some level, that the client will magically discover they can do it themselves. Believe me, if that is their best choice, they'll figure it out—usually after you've spent a lot of time and resources giving them a well-thought-out proposal. Let's get real and find out what's going on. Having asked this question many times, I find the answer falls into two broad categories: good constraints and bad constraints.

## Good Constraints

Good constraints are barriers from the past that no longer exist. The client didn't have a budget before, and now they do. They didn't have various approvals, and now they do. It wasn't a top priority, and now it is. Or they are *things the client can't do that we can*. For instance, the client says they don't have enough time, enough people, enough expertise or know-how, etc. It may not be their core competence or where they want to focus their resources. If so, they have *convinced themselves* of two things:

1. The impact is big.
2. They can't fix it themselves.

## Bad Constraints

Bad constraints are factors that have stopped success in the past and, if not changed, will stop it again in the future. Examples might be:

- They haven't been able to get this adequately budgeted.

- They can't get buy-in from the executive committee.

- The XYZ group has a vested interest in killing it.

- Politics always get in the way.

- It's been too complicated.

- They've had higher priorities.

Our question is, "What's different this time?" If nothing *is* different, it's likely nothing will *be* different. It is critical to understand what prevented the adoption of the solution in the past that will prevent it again. Often the success of the solution will change from the underlying value proposition to removing the constraints. Hitting one of these constraints is a yellow light. We can say something like, "I have a concern. It sounds like even if we come up with the best possible solution, even if it would really get you the results we discussed, it won't be adopted. Politics have killed it in the past and they will this time too. What do you think we should do?"

Frequently the client will say a version of, "Could you help us?" Just as a client will pay us to get the right evidence or to quantify the impact, they will pay us to help remove a constraint. It is high value-added. They know the impact is big and they know they won't achieve the opportunity unless the constraints are removed. If the constraints can't be removed, can they be managed or circumvented? If not, do we want to proceed? Two things are vulnerable: the solution *adoption* (their decision to go with the solution), and the solution *execution* (how well we can implement the solution and make it work).

**Opportunity**
Constraints

## CONSTRAINT CHALLENGE

In your next several client dialogues, when you sense the impact is big, ask the constraints question.

**Opportunity**
Constraints

# 16
# The Opportunity

Take Away the Solution

To this point, we've done our best for the client with each of these objectives:

☑ Move off the solution.

☑ Get out all of the issues.

☑ Develop evidence and impact.

☑ Explore context and constraints.

## When the Impact Is Small

At any point in our discussions with the client, either one of us might reach the conclusion that the impact of the opportunity is not substantial. The dollar value may not be great relative to the client's priorities or relative to the size of our typical engagement. On a scale of 1 to 10, the client is on the lower end of the scale. Or perhaps the client tries to convince us the impact isn't a big deal, thinking it is a good negotiating ploy.

**Take Away the Solution**

For whatever reason, if we sense the opportunity is either not important or is not urgent, we can exercise two choices:

1. Say so.
2. Take away the solution.

It might sound something like this: "Tom, if this problem is only costing you $100,000 a year, the problem may be cheaper than the solution. Let's say you did nothing, and just watched this over the next couple of years—would anyone even care?" or, "Linda, if this is only a 5, doesn't it seem likely that the company would be better off spending its money on 8s, 9s, and 10s?" or, "You've been working with XYZ for five years. They are a good company. Why not stay with them?" or, "It sounds like there is a huge downside if this fails. Is it possible to eliminate the risk by just not doing the project?" or, "It sounds like this is something you could handle very well in-house. Would there be any reason not to do that?"

Taking away the solution may seem counterintuitive. I say that after watching countless consultants attempt valiantly to convince the client that the impact is much more important or urgent than the client perceives it to be. This may in fact be true, and I'll deal with that situation shortly. Even if the client doesn't perceive it to be very impactful, it is much more powerful for the client to convince themselves than for us to begin efforting. Let's give them a chance. Remember our rule for yellow lights: If you hear it, see it, or feel it, find a way to say it—tactfully.

## Likely Reactions

When you take away the solution, the client is apt to do one of
two things:

1. Let it go.
2. Fight for it.

If they decide to let it go, did you lose the business? You can't lose
something you never had. You were likely to lose the business anyway; you just would have made your loss more expensive.

If they fight for it, *they have to convince you* to propose the solution
rather than you convincing them. The old cliché is, "If they say it, it's
gold; if you say it, it's sold." The corollary dictum is, "People love to
buy, they hate to be sold." It is sometimes amusing to see the consultant try to talk the client out of doing something that on the surface doesn't make sense, while the client comes up with more and
more reasons for moving ahead. Amusing or not, it is often effective.

Remember that intent counts more than technique. If your intent is to
get a solution that exactly meets the client's needs, to be authentic,
and to stay attuned with what is showing up rather than what you
would like to hear, you will be able to take away the solution and be
thoroughly congruent. A colleague of mine says, "If you aren't ready
to walk, you're not ready to talk."

The following is not the best example of taking away the solution, and I'll give it anyway—mostly because it was fun. At the time of this story, one of my responsibilities as head of a computer systems company was to get movement (regardless if it was yes or no) on opportunities that seemed to be going nowhere. After a certain amount of time of nondecision, I would intervene. I figured a "no" decision was superior to not deciding at all. If the client couldn't say yes, at least they could say no. Take note that at this time in my career, I wasn't very skilled at price negotiation. I'll correct some of my errors shown here when we talk about price negotiation later in the book.

We were working with a client on a $250,000 computer system solution. When I arrived, right from the beginning I was asking, "Wait a minute, what's causing you to even think you need a system in the first place?" So we talked through all of the issues, evidence, and impact, and he was doing a better job of convincing me he needed the system than I was of convincing him he didn't. Toward the end, he asked me for a 10 percent discount. At that point I said, "Look, you know price is not the issue here. Even if we agreed on the price, you wouldn't agree to this deal today." He said, "Yes I would." I said, "No you wouldn't." He said, "Yes I would." I said, "You don't understand what I mean. I have to leave for the airport in 20 minutes. Agreeing to the deal means you give me a check for $30,000 before I head to that plane, and you're not prepared to do that." He said, "I am too!" I said, "There's no way you'll give me a check in 20 minutes for $30,000. We don't even have a contract." He yells through the

door, "Louise, bring me my checkbook!" He wrote me a check. I said, "You're right and I was wrong. You really surprised me—I apologize. I hope I wasn't rude." Our company still had to come up with a solution that exactly met their needs, and if I thought we couldn't, I wouldn't have taken the check. Still, it felt good to have movement rather than stagnation. So, if it seems a little counterintuitive to take away the solution, often it's exactly the thing to do.

If it makes good sense for us to do business, let's work together, have fun, and make some money. If not, let's find out quickly, shake hands, and part friends.

## When the Impact Is Not Agreed Upon

It might be that the client is willing to give up the solution and you think they are making a mistake. You see the impact as being greater than they do. After all, you are an expert, and they don't know what they don't know. At this point, you have little to lose—if they don't change their perception of the impact, you won't be able to help them. It is appropriate at this point to ask some leading questions and/or give them the information you think they lack.

Let's look at the turnover problem again. Let's say you uncover the fact that they have 40 percent turnover in a key segment of their workforce. You happen to know that the industry standard (presumed evidence) is 20 percent. You ask them about the impact of having 20 percent more turnover than their competition, and they say they aren't concerned. When you ask them why not, they say that

people who have been around for a long time become both cynical and expensive. New people are cheaper and more enthusiastic. They like the 40 percent turnover. You say, "Well you might be right. Do you mind if I ask you a few questions based on my experience?"

Or you could provide them with some data about the "true cost of turnover." They will either change their perception and you will have the potential to help them, you'll change your perception and agree it's not a problem, or you'll agree to disagree. In the latter two cases, you can move on to help another client who actually feels there is a problem.

## The Map Is Not (Necessarily) the Territory

In sharing this information with clients, just because we strongly, fervently, passionately believe we are right, doesn't mean we are. Increasing our conviction doesn't make us more right. Try not to confuse certainty with reality. With that in mind, feel free to advocate what you perceive to be true, knowing that your perception is just that—your perception.

Take Away the Solution

# 17
# Immovable Solutions

## When the Client Won't Move

I said our first objective is to move off the solution. What if they won't move? What if they give us a big yellow light? Then what?

There is a difference between the client saying, "I'm looking for a sales management solution," and, "I want to implement product X." In the latter, they have already decided on the solution, and only want some help implementing it. While their choice may be "wrong," it is made. They don't want to move off the solution or even discuss it. They want to know how you will help them better or cheaper than someone else. In essence they say, "I've made my decision; do you want to play or not?"

Immovable Solutions

## Eliciting Decision Criteria

We can still provide value and attempt to find a meaningful basis for differentiation by eliciting their *criteria* for making a decision. We "structure a conversation" around two topics:

1. Their criteria for the ideal *implementation*.
2. Their criteria for the ideal solution *provider*.

In the above example, we could start out with: "Given that you know you're going with Product X, what are your criteria for an ideal *implementation* of X?" We would get out a complete list of criteria (issues) and make sure it was complete. For each issue, in order of importance, we would explore evidence and impact, and we would investigate context and constraints.

We could also ask, "What will be most important to you in terms of the *people* you work with?" We would then proceed to structure a conversation (however loosely) around those criteria as well.

## First-Order and Second-Order Needs

I call underlying business problems and results *first-order needs*. The types of questions I listed above elicit what I term *second-order needs*. These tend to be issues such as:

- **Service.** What to them is superior service?
- **Methodology.** Do they believe one methodology is superior to others?

- **Delivery** format or process. Will they want to see outcomes shown or delivered in a particular way?

- **Timing/Availability.** Can one company deliver the same results faster than others?

- **Competency.** Is one company perceived to have superior skills?

- **Compatibility.** Is one company more compatible with their culture or with their current products and processes?

- **Credibility.** Is one company more likely to do what they say?

Note that we might have a more difficult communication challenge developing evidence and impact for some of the more intangible issues. We still need to try. For instance, with service, do they have evidence of poor service in the past or present? What was the impact of getting bad service? In the future, how would they know with certainty they were getting good service? What specific measurements would they use? (If none exist, would those measurements be important? Would they like some help setting the measurements up?) What would be the real pay-off to the project and/or company if they got truly superior service? Who or what else would good or bad service affect? What has stopped them from getting excellent service in the past?

> If we can't develop **first-order needs**, we need to develop **second-order needs**, or the client will only differentiate on **price**.

If the client won't discuss *first-order needs,* and we can't differentiate ourselves on *second-order needs,* what is the one last criterion on which the client will decide? Price! And if you aren't the low-cost provider, you won't get that business. If we sense that, we might say, "I have a concern. I sense that the only criterion for this decision is price, and I'm sure someone, somehow, can come in with a lower

**Immovable Solutions**

price. Would there by any convincing justification for accepting a proposal even if it had a higher price?" At least you've given yourself, and the client, an opportunity to come back to some needs other than just price.

## IMMOVABLE SOLUTION CHALLENGE

When the client won't move off the solution, be aware of what is happening and choose to elicit decision criteria. Seek for differentiation on *second-order needs*.

# 18
# The Opportunity

Overview

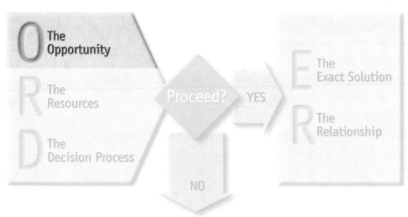

We have covered a lot of information. The risk is getting lost in the details. Let's step back for a moment and look at the big picture. All we are trying to do is gain mutual understanding around the following:

☑ **Move off the solution.** If they won't move, elicit decision criteria.

☑ **Get out all of the issues.** Problems or results the solution must resolve.

☑ **Develop evidence and impact** for each issue in order of priority or for the issues collectively.

☑ **Explore context and constraints** either by issue or for the issues collectively.

If we wanted to look at this as a list of inquiries, they would be:

1. What are all of the issues the solution is intended to resolve?
2. What's letting you know it's a problem? *Problem Evidence*
3. What is the impact on the business? *Problem Impact*
4. How would you measure success? *Result Evidence*
5. What is the payoff if success is achieved? *Result Impact*
6. Who or what else is affected? *Operational Context*
7. What is the big picture? *Organizational Context*
8. What has stopped the organization from resolving this in the past? *Constraints*
9. Did I get it right? Did I leave anything out? *Summarize*

If you wanted a worksheet to remind you of what to ask, it would look like this:

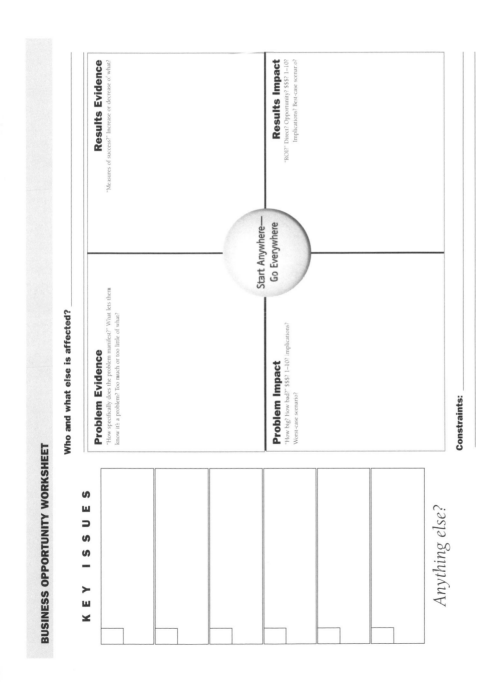

**BUSINESS OPPORTUNITY WORKSHEET**

**Who and what else is affected?**

**Results Evidence**
"Measures of success?" Increase or decrease of what?

**Results Impact**
"ROI?" Direct? Opportunity? $$$? 1–10? Implications? Best-case scenar o?

**Start Anywhere—Go Everywhere**

**Problem Evidence**
"How specifically does the problem manifest?" What lets them know it's a problem? Too much or too little of what?

**Problem Impact**
"How big? How bad?" $$$? 1–10? Implications? Worst-case scenario?

**Constraints:**

**K E Y   I S S U E S**

*Anything else?*

127

If you like flow charts, use this one:

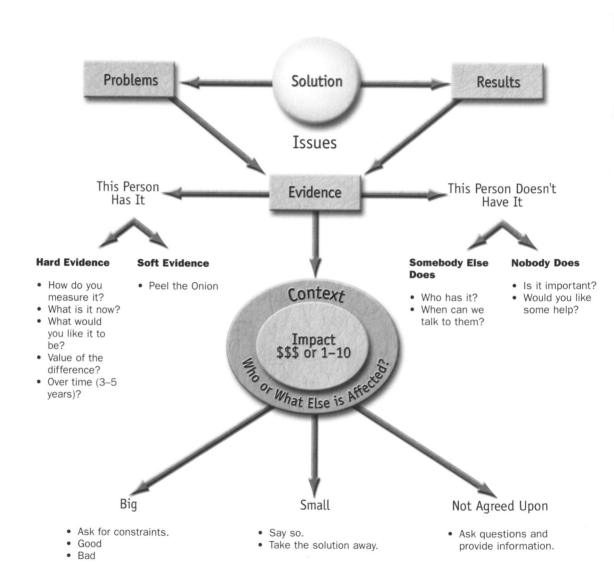

# 19
# Start Anywhere, Go Everywhere

It is hard to overemphasize the concept of "Start anywhere, go everywhere." I've presented material in a linear fashion. Life is much more random. Think of this as more of a checklist than a recipe. Like a pilot checks off each critical item before taking off, we check off *issues, evidence, impact, context,* and *constraints* before offering a solution. Unlike the pilot, we may not follow the same order every time. One of the designs of this material is to bring flexibility to some things in business development that are too inflexible, and to bring order to a process that is often chaotic. It should serve you the same way.

- If you can't get out all of the issues, go with what you have and come back later. If that's what the client wants to do, so be it.
- If you start talking about one issue and it absorbs many others, that's natural.

- If issues combine or divide or change importance, that's what the list is for. It's a dynamic list, not static.
- If you are having trouble talking about problems, flip to results, and vice versa.
- If it makes more sense to go for impact before evidence, go for it.
- If *problem evidence and impact* seem redundant with *result evidence and impact,* eliminate one of them.
- Ask the five measurement questions in any order that makes sense. (How do you measure it? What is it now? What would you like it to be? What's the value of the difference? What's the value of the difference over time?) Leave out any that don't fit.
- If constraints are the first things to show up, talk about them.
- If you want to start with the big picture, go ahead. If you finish talking about the big picture, then move to the issues.

Remember, the map is not the territory. The model is a tool to help us create mutual success. When it works, use it. When it doesn't, do what works. Use everything here with awareness and choice.

# 20
# The Resources

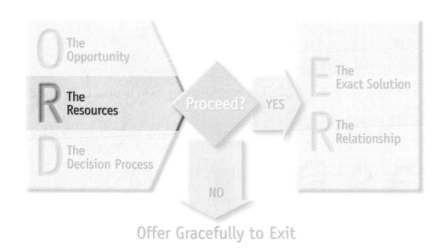

We have spent considerable time discussing how to explore the nature and size of an opportunity. You can't help someone succeed who has no problems to solve or results to achieve. Even though you've discovered what your client really needs, and the opportunity is real, you can't help them succeed if they have insufficient resources. At this stage, we're trying to get any resources (yellow lights turned to

green) up front, not afterward when it becomes much more difficult. There are three resources we want to establish before we move any further: *time, people, and money.* We have to know if there is an overlap between what they feel is necessary and available and what we feel is required in order to get a solution that truly meets their needs.

## Timing

Remember where we are in the process. We've just gone through the Opportunity, and have mutually agreed it is worth achieving. A timing question then is, "What is the date by which you hope to get these results in place?" That's often a good way to start because it allows you to work backward from what they hope to achieve to where they are right now. Or we may ask, "When were you hoping to get started?" or "What kind of time frame are we working on?" Timing is obviously not too hard of a question to ask—you just have to ask it. Make it clear that you are not pushing for commitment or trying to "close the deal." You are just finding out what works for them. Research shows that in complex sales, the use of "closing" techniques is negatively correlated with success. The old adage, "Close early and close often," seems to be dead wrong.

Your intent here is only to make sure you and your client are on the same page. Disconnects on timing include:

1. The timing is too soon.

2. The timing is too far out.

3. The timing is undefined.

Yellow lights in timing are usually at the extremes (too soon or too far

out), and they are predictable. For example, if it's too far out, you may say, "I'm confused. You said this was costing you $10 million a year, and you want to wait three years to fix it? That's $30 million down the tubes. What makes that acceptable?" You can only say something like that if you've done a good job in Opportunity (with the right intent). Otherwise, you won't know the numbers, and you won't have developed the rapport to challenge their assumption.

What if the yellow light is that they want it too soon? Find out *what's driving that date*. If the reason is truly compelling, you may break the project into phases and prioritize what should come first. If they need it that soon, and it's impossible to deliver by their date, we may have to say, "I have a concern. I think it's possible for you to get the results we talked about; I don't think it's possible within that time period. If we could really get you the results and it took three months instead of two weeks, should we keep talking?" You'll either find out the time constraint is real (and at least you found the red light early on), or the client is prepared to trade timing for money or for breaking the project into phases.

## People

People, or division of labor, means we are trying to find out what their beliefs are about the proper roles of their company and ours— about what work they'll do and what work we'll do. This is at a high level. We are not trying to get into the specific details or daily efforts. We are looking for yellow lights, and again, they are at the extremes—either they want too little of their involvement or too

much of their involvement.

**Too little of their involvement.** Our concern is they may not give us the key people internally that we need to be successful. "I have a concern. Unless we can get participation by top management, the project may very well fail. What can we do to get it?"

**Too much of their involvement.** If they want to do critical parts of the project themselves, we may be concerned that they won't commit the necessary time, quality, or expertise. This is particularly important if our performance is dependent on them doing a good job. We can say, "Help me understand how you view the responsibility for this project. Are you hoping we'll manage the project and you'll subcontract your people to us, or are you going to be fully responsible for management and subcontract us?" If they want us to take responsibility for it, then we will want the authority to manage their people as we would manage our own people. Anybody who is not putting in either the time or quality we expect can be taken off the project and replaced with someone more capable. And there is a management fee for directing their people just as there is for directing ours.

## Money

To this point we've checked off time and people. We now come to my favorite: money. It always seems the energy level picks up when we finally start talking to the client about money. Suddenly you can feel molecules vibrating at a higher frequency.

There are two times you'll need to talk about money. One is now, in

Resources, and the other is later in Exact Solution. At this stage, we're only talking about *value* justification. We're not going to give them our fees or price, and we're not asking them for the specific dollars they have in a budget. We're trying to understand if there is congruence between what they think it's *worth* to solve the problem and what we think is *necessary* to solve the problem. In the Exact Solution step, when we actually present our proposal and give them a price, we will talk *price* negotiation—are they getting the best deal?

The question of "Are we getting the best deal?" (price negotiation) is very different than "Can we afford this?" (value justification), and it is important to understand the difference. Here is a quick example. Let's say you're looking to buy a new car. One of the first economic decisions you make is the dollar range you can afford to spend on a car. When you actually go into the marketplace, your price range may budge, but fundamentally you have some notion of the worth of a vehicle to you. Let's say you decide you can spend $30,000. You find the vehicle you really want and it costs $30,000. Now what do you do? You bargain! The issue is not whether you can afford to spend $30,000—you've already figured that out. The issue becomes are you getting the best deal? All we are trying to find out from the client in Resources is their belief about worth, about value. If we can't get over this hurdle, talking specific price is moot.

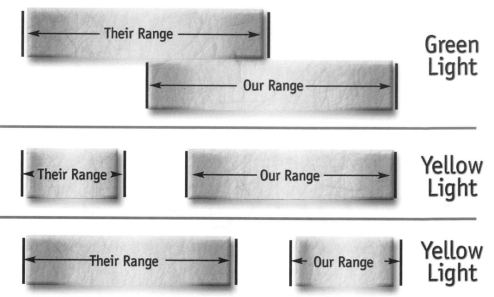

Remember, intent counts more than technique. Our intent is to just figure out if we are both headed in the same direction and if we should keep going. If not, let's find out now so we don't waste each other's time. There is a price below which people would not reasonably expect to get good quality, and there's a price above which you could add features and benefits for the rest of your life, and it wouldn't make any difference to them. They have a range. It may not be explicit or conscious, and it's there. And we have a range too. The question is whether their range is going to overlap with our range. If it's not, we probably can't do business.

I've seen consultants spend more in direct and opportunity costs on the proposal than the client had in their budget for the solution, and they never knew it was happening. They could have found that out in about two minutes.

If you walk out of a meeting with a client and you don't know how much they are thinking of spending, and they don't know how much you are thinking of charging, you are both guessing. No guessing! The first time you test your price with that client should not be when you present your proposal. It is too costly and too unnecessary to guess.

So here is our money question: *"Have you established a budget for this project?"* We're not asking what their budget is—only whether they have established a budget. There are some predictable responses to the money question:

**Yes.**

And they can't/won't share it with us.

And it seems sufficient.

And it's too small.

And it's too big. (We wish!)

**No.**

You tell me how much it will cost.

Money's no problem. (Or, "If it's worth it, we'll come up with the money.")

I don't know. (Someone else knows or no one knows.)

Others?

These responses are finite and predictable. Because they are finite and predictable, we should have some predictable responses. They received their script at "client school," and we should have the other page.

# The "Three-Part Response"

We are not negotiating, so it doesn't matter who goes first. What matters is finding out if we are in the same ballpark. Commit to memory your version of this three-part response:

1. "I don't know how much this will cost you." (Every client situation is unique.)
2. "However, other companies in similar situations—trying to get the results you've been talking about—tend to invest between X and Y."
3. "Can you see yourself falling somewhere in that range?"

Notice here we haven't said, "We charge other companies…." We are just saying other companies in similar situations, trying to get these results, whether they do it with us or with a competitor or by themselves, tend to invest between X and Y. And Y should be between about 25 to 50 percent more than X. Saying, "Somewhere between $100,000 and $10,000,000," is not a meaningful range. Saying, "Between $200,000 to $250,000" works.

When we give them the range, we usually will get one of two responses:

1. "Yes" (however grudgingly).
2. "Oh my goodness, that's way more than we were thinking." (We just wanted this project. We didn't want to buy your whole company.) That's at least a yellow light.

We just want to find out if our ranges overlap or if their chair is going to fall over when we put out something reasonable. We would rather have their chair fall over now than after we've committed a lot of our company's resources to a proposal that won't make sense to the client.

In your initial conversations with the client, you may not have a realistic range in mind; you may not want to give out a number without further input from your colleagues. If so, get the client's permission to go back and work with your team a bit, get a sense for where the proposal might head economically, and call them back for guidance. When you call them back with a range, they can tell you to either keep working, or to stop the presses because you're thinking of two radically different numbers. All we're going to do with our team is run some rough numbers. We're not going to have everybody run around and develop a big proposal when we have no idea what the client is willing to spend. Let's see how the three-part response is applied.

### No. We don't have a budget.

If they say, "No we haven't," we say, "How are you planning to fund this project?" We say it nicely. Remember to ask hard questions in a soft way. Or we ask, "What were your expectations?" Interestingly, having done this enough times, they tend to default to one of these other predictable responses: "Well, we won't know until we have some proposals," or "You tell me," or "Money's not an issue," etc.

We could also say, "Let's bat around some numbers so you have something to work with. At this point:

1. "I don't know how much this will cost you." (Every client situation is unique.)

2. "However, other companies in similar situations—trying to get the results you've been talking about—tend to invest between X and Y."

3. "Can you see yourself falling somewhere in that range?"

### You tell me.

The client says some version of, "You're the expert. You tell me how much this will cost."

We might say, "That's fair enough. At this point:

1. "I don't know how much this will cost you." (Every client situation is unique.)

2. "However, other companies in similar situations—trying to get the results you've been talking about—tend to invest between X and Y."

3. "Can you see yourself falling somewhere in that range?"

### Money's no problem.

And what if they say, "Oh, money's not an issue. We'll come up with the money. Just give us a proposal, prove that it's worth it, and we'll come up with the money." Our three-part response will serve us well again. We might say, "Well that's good to hear. Just so there are no surprises, at this point:

1. "I don't know how much this will cost you." (Every client situation is unique.)

**Resources**

2. "However, other companies in similar situations—trying to get the results you've been talking about—tend to invest between X and Y."

3. "Can you see yourself falling somewhere in that range?"

By the way, money is *always* an issue.

## I can't tell you.

Now what if they say, "I'd rather not tell you what we have in mind," or "I'm not allowed to tell you; that's against our policy"? Once again, we are well served by our three-part response. We say, "You know, that's not a problem. I don't want you to do anything you're not comfortable with. I don't really need a specific number anyway. Let *me* throw out some numbers and get your reaction. Right now:

1. "I don't know how much this will cost you." (Every client situation is unique.)

2. "However, other companies in similar situations—trying to get the results you've been talking about—tend to invest between X and Y."

3. "Can you see yourself falling somewhere in that range?"

## I don't know.

They give us some version of "I don't know." It's fair to ask, "That's not a problem. Who would know?" Notice that the budget discussion is positioned right before the Decision Process. That's because a discussion of money often involves other people and processes. Even if we find out who else we need to talk to, we can still try out the three-part response on this person and get a preliminary reaction.

141

## And How Did You Come Up with That Number?

We are left with two situations: (1) they have a budget and it's too small, (2) we give them a range and they don't fit into it. For whatever reason, their expected expenditure is less than ours. Anytime they come up with a number that's smaller than your number—if you can stop the panicky feeling in your being, if your ego hasn't rushed in from the door to save you, and if you have composure—say, "*And how did you come up with that number?*"

This is an important question. You'll find the response will often fall into one of two buckets: logistics or value. You don't want to be fighting a *value* battle if the reason is logistics, and you don't want to fight a *logistics* battle if the reason is value. The way you find out is by asking, "And how did you come up with that number?"

## Logistics or Value?

Logistics would be something like "That's all we have left in this year's budget." Then we want to find out what that number is and how much they have in *next* year's budget. They're not saying it isn't worth

LOGISTICS   VALUE

it, they're just saying they have some logistical constraints. They may also say, "Well that's all I'm authorized to spend." That's fine. Who's authorized to spend the larger amount? Or they may say, "That's all we have to get started."

We might respond, "Great. Let's say we get started and are success-ful—where would the rest of the money come from?" Once again, they are not arguing about the value of doing it, they're just worried about the logistics.

Value, on the other hand, is some version of "That's all we think it's worth." We clearly have a yellow light, so we may as well deal with it. We might say, "Well I appreciate you sharing that information. I have a concern. I really think it's possible to get you the results you're talk-ing about. I don't think it's possible for less than $250,000 to $300,000 dollars. Give me some guidance; does that mean you would not want us to give you a proposal?"

If they say, "Yes, we still want you to give us a proposal," then we're still confused, and we state it: "I'm confused. It sounds to me that even if I came in with the best possible solution, and you were con-vinced this was better than anything else you could do, you wouldn't buy it because your budget is less than what I'm going to come in with. What do you think we should do?" Amazingly enough, they often find a way to come up with the money.

If they say, "Don't bother proposing if that's what you'll come in with," our yellow light is threatening to go to red. It's helpful to remember where we are. The value of the solution is much higher than the numbers we are putting out. *So it's not a question of money, it's a question of belief.* It's usually one of three things:
1. They don't believe in the *value* you discussed.

2. They don't believe that *what you do* will give them that value.

3. They believe they can get the *same value somewhere else for less.* Otherwise they would do it. It should be a "no-brainer" based on a value that is far greater than the investment.

We have to uncover the belief that's stopping them from doing something that seems to make sense. So we ask them: "Frank, usually when we get to this point in the conversation, and we're so far apart on the value of a project, I find one of three things is happening. Either:

- "You don't believe in the value we discussed,

- "You don't believe that what we do will give provide that value,

- "Or you believe you can get the same value somewhere else for less. Is one of those three things happening?"

If they don't really believe the numbers we developed in the Opportunity discussion, we might say, "Well, if I didn't have confidence in the return, I'd question the investment myself. Let's revisit our numbers and see what you think is more realistic."

If they have some reason to doubt that what we do will give them the desired results, we say "I'm glad you're willing to say so. If I had doubts, I'd probably question any investment. Let's talk about your concerns."

If they have reason to believe they can get the same results somewhere else for less, then let's get real. If they truly feel they can get the same results for less money, they should do it. It's a no-brainer. If they

didn't do it, they would be fiscally irresponsible. If we were sitting in their shoes, what's the only question we might have? Are they really going to get the same results? Is it an apples-to-apples comparison? We should make sure it is. Let's say it as it is:

Client: "I think I can get the same results for less money."

Consultant: "If you can, you should. If I were sitting in your shoes, and I could get the exact same results for less money, I'd be fiscally irresponsible not to do it. I completely respect that. I guess the only way you could get burned is if you were not really comparing apples to apples—if what another company thought they were delivering for your money is not the same result we're talking about. I'll tell you what I'd be willing to do. Do you have a proposal from someone else?"

Client: "Yes."

Consultant: "I'd be willing to invest a half hour of my time. Let's go over the proposal together. I don't want you to show me anything proprietary—just the scope; just what they say they are going to do. If what they are going to do is the same as what we have in mind, I'll advise you to go with them. If I see some radical differences, I'll point them out. You might still go with them. At least you'll make a well-informed decision. Does that sound reasonable?"

If they don't have a proposal, we can inquire how they came up with their belief. If they say they are going to get a proposal, we say, "Great. When you get the proposal, I'd be willing to invest…," and we use the same rationale.

If they ask us to just send in our proposal and they'll judge, then we may have a problem. We are unwilling to send in a proposal that seems doomed to failure. We might say something like, "Susan, if I hear you right, you believe someone else can deliver the same results I can for less money. Basically, you're telling me not to propose. I'd be happy to propose if we could come up with a reason that would really make a difference—a strong justification for spending more money with us than with another party. If we can't come up with that reason, it seems like I'd be wasting both our companies' time. What's your sense?"

Remember, our intent is to get a solution that exactly meets the client's needs. It's impossible to take fiscal realities out of that analysis. If we come back with a solution that is 10 times what they can afford, we haven't helped them or ourself. If the first time we try out an invest-ment amount with the client is when they hear our presentation or read our proposal, we are guessing. And the cost of guessing could be very high.

If we are going to hit a yellow light, now is a good time to deal with it. We have just finished the Opportunity step and have agreed that the impact is big. Otherwise, we wouldn't be here. They haven't even

heard our solution. If we have developed rapport and added value with our diagnosis, they want to see what we will come up with. They don't get to see it if we can't get some agreement on worth. We still have leverage, and they still have motivation. If we can't get past this juncture, at least we haven't made failure more expensive. We will have more time to spend with clients where the fit is good.


## RESOURCES CHALLENGE

Don't go into the Exact Solution step without qualifying the client on time, people, and money. Especially money!

**Resources**

# 21
# The Decision Process

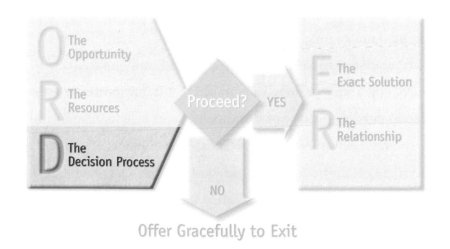

In the Opportunity step, I said you can't help people succeed who have no problems to solve or results to achieve. Even if there is a qualified opportunity, you can't help someone with insufficient resources. Here we take it one step further and say: Even if there is a big *opportunity* with sufficient *resources*, you can't help someone succeed who can't make a *decision*. How often have you done a great job of presenting a solution to someone who couldn't buy? How often have you made a

presentation or proposal to people whose criteria for judging you were unknown to you—perhaps unknown to them as well?

Getting good at developing a *mutual* understanding of the decision process, people, and criteria is not easy. Few consultants seem to do it well. Many dysfunctional buying practices tend to complicate the mere attempt. A litany of complaints ensue:

- Our sales cycles are too long; it is very costly, and we have a hard time intelligently allocating resources.
- We spend huge amounts of time and money on deals where we didn't have a realistic chance or someone else was a "lock."
- We spend a ton of time and money, and *nobody* gets the business.
- We have to fill out time-consuming RFPs with numerous questions that don't seem to relate to a solution that would really meet the client's needs—and nothing happens.
- We're not allowed to talk to the key decision makers, and they are surprised when they don't get a proposal that critically addresses their key issues.
- Clients sometimes treat consultants as if they were a commodity, as if proposals would do the work and the people were completely interchangeable.
- Clients want us to go to bidders' conferences and share our analytical approach with everyone else—to do our competition's work for them.
- We answer all their questions, give them our best thinking, share how we would do the work, and they use the information to do it themselves.

Could you add to the list?

*Because it is challenging to elicit and articulate the decision process, the few who do it well will distance themselves from the competition.* They will offer value to the client and tremendously increase their ability to come up with a solution that is adopted and which really works. They will leverage time and allocate resources more efficiently and effectively.

## What Do We Want to Know?

We are not likely to find something if we don't know what we are looking for. Let's say I am a client and I promise to tell you honestly and accurately anything you want to know about my company's decision process. What would you ask? Here's a partial compilation of what I've heard from consultants in response to that question:

- Who is going to make the decision?
- Who is going to influence the decision?
- Who can veto the decision?
- Who signs the check?
- Who approves the decision?
- Who is involved in the decision?
- What are the criteria for a yes decision?
- Can I have the business?
- What's the process?
- How will the decision be made?
- What information do you need?
- When are you going to make the decision?
- Who is the competition?

- How do I stack up against the competition?
- What do I have to do to win?
- Are you sure you'll go with *someone*?

## How Do We Get This Information?

I have seen consultants (me included) flail away at getting answers to the above questions, with spotty success. I suggest that having a structure and sequence of questions for eliciting this information greatly increases your likelihood of getting it. After many years of observation and real-world testing, I'll offer an approach that works well. As always, use it with awareness and choice. If you have anything better, use it. (And tell me what it is.)

We're first going to find out what the *steps* are to making the decision. Next, we're going to find out what *decision* gets made in each step. (Sometimes these first two are the same, and sometimes they're different.) And we'll find out *when* they will decide. Then we're going to find out *who* is involved in each step, and *how* they will decide (what it will take for them to say yes or no). One of our key outcomes in this process will be to *find out the "how" directly from the "who."*

When we talk to the *"who,"* we're going to find out the issues from their perspective and their *criteria* for making the decision. Among those criteria will be how they will decide between *alternative solutions* (the competition), *who is perceived to win or lose* if this is adopted, and their *personal stake* in the success or failure of this intervention.

**Decision Process**

Collecting this information is called "working the grid." If you want to shorten your sales cycle, this is where you're going to make it happen. You'll have a manageable list of steps. You'll know that when you get to the end of those steps, something happens, whether it's a yes or a no. You should have a composite sense of a solution that would truly work. You should at least be aware of dysfunctional buying practices and whether the deck is stacked unfairly against you. Although you may not win, you should be able to decide whether this game is real and if—or how—you want to play.

## The Steps

The first question we ask is, "What are the steps?" What are the steps the client will take internally in order to decide? We are looking for a discrete series of go/no-go events that culminate in a final decision in which the client has confidence.

**What are the steps?**

**THE DECISION PROCESS**

| Steps | Decision | When | Who | How |
|-------|----------|------|-----|-----|
| Talk to 6–8 companies | | | | |
| Narrow to 3 | | | | |
| Pass on to Selection Committee | | | | |
| Refer to CEO | | | | |

There is a reason we start with the steps rather than the "who." Here's

the first problem in starting out with the "who." Being innocent consultants, the temptation is to get right to it and just ask, "So who's really going to make this decision?" with the unspoken message of, "Clearly it's not you. You're not important." The second problem is when you ask people, "So who's really going to make this decision?" what do they most often say? "I am." Which, even if it is partially true, is not often accurate.

I read the case of purchasing behavior regarding a very expensive heating and air-conditioning system for large buildings. An independent research company sent out a questionnaire to plant managers, maintenance managers, executive vice-presidents, the CFO and the CEO, etc. The questionnaire said, "Who is *really*, ultimately responsible for this purchasing decision?" The answer came back, "I am," from all of those different people. There is no sense in repeatedly asking questions that do not elicit the information we need. So we start with the steps rather than the "who."

We need to find, in essence, the steps they would have to take internally to figure out if the solution makes sense, or if there are better uses for their money. These steps should allow them to feel completely confident in saying *either* yes or no. A decision not to decide is a decision, and usually a suboptimal one. *To get good information about what it takes to get a yes, make no be an okay answer.* When people really feel that no is an acceptable answer, they'll give you good information. As soon as they feel you're trying to pin them down and lead them to your conclusion, the trust alarm will go off loud and clear

**To get good information about what it takes to get a yes, make no be an okay answer.**

and you'll get less complete, less accurate information.

Steps are also a fairly neutral, impersonal place to start; there is often not a lot of emotional baggage. For example:

- We're going to talk to maybe six to eight companies.
- We're going to narrow that down to about three companies.
- We're going to pass those three on to our selection committee.
- We might refer it up to the CEO just to get her blessing.

We might test the list to make sure they didn't leave anything out. Our experience may tell us that others affected by the decision will have some input. We might say, "Won't you have to get some user buy-in for this?" They may say, "Yes, they're on the selection committee," or "Well yes, of course." And we'll ask where that fits in their decision process. Or perhaps they say, "No, not on this project." That may be a yellow light for us to check out. Once we have scrutinized the list for likely completeness and accuracy, we've got a series of steps.

## Be Proactive—The Steps

If there are no steps, if the steps seem insufficient for a good decision, or if you feel beforehand that you know a series of steps that would serve the process well, suggest them. There is nothing wrong with filling in a vacuum.

**Decision Process**

**What decision gets made**

**in each step?**

# The Decision

## THE DECISION PROCESS

| Steps | Decision | When | Who | How |
|---|---|---|---|---|
| Talk to 6–8 companies | Which 6–8? | | | |
| Narrow to 3 | Which 3? Defend choices | | | |
| Pass on to Selection Committee | Recommend top choice and defend | | | |
| Refer to CEO | Confirm or push back | | | |

The next question we need answered is, "What decisions get made at each step?" I find this question often ignored. Sometimes the "step" and the decision are the same: "The standards committee will check for compliance and state their opinion." Sometimes the decision is unclear. In the example shown here, when three companies are "passed on" to the selection committee, what decision is made? Is it "Here are the pros and cons of the three; you decide," or "Here is the one we recommend and here is our justification"? If they have a selection committee, what would be the reason for sending it to the CEO? What decision really gets made at that step? Does the CEO just rubber-stamp the committee's decision, or does she really look to punch holes in the recommendation? Is she going to look for more information, or just confirm? Our goal is to clearly and explicitly understand "What specifically do these people decide or influence in this step?"

156

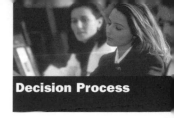
# Be Proactive—The Decision

If you feel there are critical decisions necessary for good, critical thinking…suggest them.

**THE DECISION PROCESS**

| Steps | Decision | When | Who | How |
|---|---|---|---|---|
| Talk to 6–8 companies | Which 6–8? | May 15–June 1 | | |
| Narrow to 3 | Which 3? Defend choices | June 8 | | |
| Pass on to Selection Committee | Recommend top choice and defend | June 15 | | |
| Refer to CEO | Confirm or push back | June 22–26 | | |

**When will they decide?**

# The When

Next we find out when. Each go/no-go decision should have a date on it. This becomes a manageable "up-front agreement" between you and the client. You'll both know when you walk through this process that the client will be able to say yes or no with confidence. We certainly won't be surprised if things change. We won't be surprised if the grid is modified as we talk to other stakeholders. If we can remain explicit and in mutual agreement about the changes and modifications, if we "work the grid," we will definitely shorten our business-development cycle. We will help clients make better decisions in their own best interest.

## Be Proactive—The When

If timelines are missing or fuzzy, suggest some. Keep in mind that we often want the client to decide on our timetable rather than theirs. Choose milestones that would seem reasonable to you if you were the client.

**Who gets involved in each step?**

## The Who

We have three columns completed now: the steps, what decisions get made in those steps, and when those decisions will be made. The fourth question we ask is, "Who's involved in each step?"

**THE DECISION PROCESS**

| Steps | Decision | When | Who | How |
|-------|----------|------|-----|-----|
| Talk to 6–8 companies | Which 6–8? | May 15–June 1 | Me | |
| Narrow to 3 | Which 3? Defend choices | June 8 | Me, end user, 1 Unit Head | |
| Pass on to Selection Committee | Recommend top choice and defend | June 15 | CFO, CIO, EVP, 4 Unit Heads | |
| Refer to CEO | Confirm or push back | June 22–26 | CEO | |

At this point, we're not asking what each person's role is or the reasons they're involved in this step. We're going to talk to those people directly and find out what they do and how they see things. All we want from the person we're talking to is who's involved in the steps. Later on, based on our direct conversations, we might state our understanding of the person's role.

Some typical roles would be:

- **Initiator.** Opens the transaction.
- **Gatekeeper.** Controls information flow and access.
- **Champion.** Willing and able to grant access to decision makers.
- **Influencer.** Nonbuyer who affects the purchase—from inside or outside the organization.
- **User.** Affected directly by the purchase.
- **Decision Maker.** Makes the decision to buy.
- **Ratifier.** Approves the decision to buy.

The roles listed are often inclusive, not exclusive. People often take on many roles in the decision process. In complex opportunities, it is often helpful to have an organizational chart—either formal or one created with your counterparts.

## Ratifier or Closet Decision Maker?

I find that one of the most difficult things to figure out is whether somebody's a ratifier or a decision maker. For example, if the CEO is *truly* a ratifier, we don't need to see her. She's probably just going to rubber-stamp it. The *real* decision makers are going to be on the selection committee. If she *is* going to make the final decision, we've got to see her or we'll be guessing about the solution. It's often hard to decide which is which, and a wrong decision can be problematic.

I was working with a company that was trying to decide between a well-known competitor and us. The paradigm of the competitor was "Start at the top, stay at the top." They would only talk to the execu-

tive vice-president. It turned out that the EVP had a higher organizational role, but a subordinate buying role—he had truly delegated the buying decision to somebody else. The person who had the buying decision didn't feel particularly respected by these people who wouldn't talk to her. I could well imagine it affected her decision to choose us. Don't confuse organizational authority with buying authority. In today's world they don't always equate.

In working on a seven-figure opportunity, one of our competitors' paradigms was "Get to the economic buyer." They misjudged a companywide executive group as the "economic buyer" (I could understand their confusion; we couldn't figure out who the real buyer was either), and decided to withdraw when they couldn't meet with them. The odds went from one of three competitors to one of two, and we were chosen. We made a gut call, and in this case it served us well.

I have also seen consultants (me included) spend months on an opportunity only to have the true decision maker—someone who had never been interviewed—dispose of the analysis in two minutes. Often the feedback loop on our decisions is short and painful. And thus, hopefully, we learn greater awareness and more choices.

One question I sometimes ask is, "Of the last ten times you sent a recommendation to X, how many times did they go against it or pass it back for more scrutiny?" If they say, "four or five," then they are decision makers. If they say, "Maybe one, if ever," then they are ratifiers.

## Be Proactive—The Who

If you feel there are key stakeholders who are critical to the decision process who have not been mentioned, suggest them.

**How will they decide?**

## The How

**THE DECISION PROCESS**

| Steps | Decision | When | Who | How |
|---|---|---|---|---|
| Talk to 6–8 companies | Which 6–8? | May 15 – June 1 | Me | Elicit now |
| Narrow to 3 | Which 3? Defend choices | June 8 | Me, end user, 1 Unit Head | Talk to each |
| Pass on to Selection Committee | Recommend top choice and defend | June 15 | CFO, CIO, EVP, 4 Unit Heads | Talk to each |
| Refer to CEO | Confirm or push back | June 22–26 | CEO | Talk to each |

Next we find out the "how" directly from the "who." Our goal is to *never make a presentation or a proposal to people whose criteria for judging you are unknown to you.* No guessing. The best way to understand what is important to the key stakeholders is to talk to them. And here is where we often get blocked. Finding out the "how" directly from the "who" is so important and so challenging that we'll spend the next chapter on it. Please hold on for just a bit.

**Our goal is to never make a presentation or a proposal to people whose criteria for judging us are unknown to us.**

**Get the "how" directly from the "who."**

When we get to see these people, we want to know ORD from *their* perspective—or put another way, the issues from their perspective and their criteria for making the decision. Among the criteria are

their discriminations among alternative solutions (competition) who they feel will win or lose if the project proceeds, and their personal stake in the success or failure of the solution. To all of these, we will return shortly.

## Be Proactive—The How

It is very common that decision criteria will be missing or not be well thought out. Based on your experience, you may be able to suggest criteria that would be helpful. Again, don't be afraid to fill in the vacuum.

## The Hard Part

The hard part is making sure we get access to all the people we need to see, and to create value when we talk to them. Let's generate some ideas.

# 22
# The Decision Process

The "How" From the "Who"

## How You Sell Is a Free Sample of How You Solve

It is difficult, if not impossible, to meet the needs of people you've never talked to. And for clients, how you "sell" is a free sample of how you solve. If they don't get to see how you analyze a problem and how you work with them in person, it is harder to decide between you and other consultants. In an ideal world, it is better for us to talk, and yet the world is not ideal. Buyers often feel abused by either manipulative or incompetent consultants. You are a buyer—have you felt that way? As a result, dysfunctional buying practices have arisen to combat dysfunctional selling practices. *You are guilty until proven innocent.*

Buyers would rather have a "less than optimal" solution than be aggravated by ignorance, arrogance, or incompetence. As a result, the norm is, "Don't let them get to me, don't let them waste my time." If

**It is difficult, if not impossible, to meet the needs of people you've never talked to.**

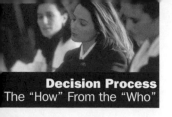

we are good at our profession, *not* getting to them *is* a waste of time—for both of us.

## Tell, Don't Ask

Business development is a balance between inquiry (seeking first to understand) and advocacy (seeking to be understood). Trying to meet with the people making the decision is a point where we switch from inquiry to advocacy. Don't bother asking, "Can I see the people who will be making the decision?" It's like walking into the doctor's office and testing reflexes.

| | |
|---|---|
| You: | "Can I talk to those other people who are making the decision, too?" |
| Them: | "No." |
| You: | "Oh. Well, can I talk to the two end users and the unit business head who are going to decide how you narrow the competition?" |
| Them: | "No." |
| You: | "What about the selection committee, can I talk to the members of the selection committee?" |
| Them: | "No." |
| You: | "And of course, can I talk to the CEO?" |
| Them: | "No." |

The reflexes are strong and predictable. The policies and behaviors are working perfectly, it's just that they're perfectly dysfunctional. So you don't ask at this point, you tell. And you can "tell" because your

only goal is to get a solution that exactly meets your client's needs. The people on the selection committee are clearly key owners of those needs, and to meet their needs, you'll need to talk to them. Your client will know better than you how to make that happen, so listen to their suggestions.

In fact, that is exactly what we might say: "Our goal is to get you a solution that exactly meets your needs. From what you described to me, the members of the selection committee are key owners of those needs. To make any kind of intelligent proposal, I'll need to talk to them. You know the company better than I do. How do we make that happen?"

## Reciprocity—The Equivalence of Actions

The client is likely to ask us to spend considerable resources on developing and presenting a solution. The assumption is that the effort we put in is of value to them. If not, why bother? All we are asking of them is a value exchange, a quid pro quo, an equivalence of actions. We will happily put in the time to develop and present our ideas, even with no guarantee of winning, as long as they will give us access to the information necessary to make those ideas relevant and meaningful. If we are willing to put in *a lot* of time in diagnosis and prescription, are the individuals on their side willing to invest *a little* time (20 to 30 minutes each) in mutually understanding their priorities? If not, when does the magic green light of trust and cooperation necessary for successful solutions get turned on?

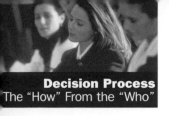
## Yellow Lights

If the client won't let us talk to the key stakeholders, refuses any equivalence of actions, or wants us to spend a lot of time, people, and money merely guessing, then that is a yellow light. Once again, we may hear ourselves say something like:

1. I have a concern.

2. I'm confused.

3. I think we may have a problem.

We state the nature of our concern. If there are several people involved in the decision, it is our assumption they're involved because they each bring a different perspective on the problems, the results, the issues, the evidence, the impact, the context, the constraints, the necessary resources, the decision criteria, etc. Our concern is that unless we understand this information directly from these people, we're likely to give them a proposal that makes absolutely no sense—and that's completely off target; it serves no one well. Even in the best case, we'll waste their time and they won't make a good decision in the best interest of their company. Worst-case scenario, it might needlessly and inappropriately kill the project. All we are asking is for 20 to 30 minutes with each one of them, and we can do it over the phone. We ask, "Isn't that reasonable?" Isn't it?

## Predictable Responses

Just because we tell, and don't ask, doesn't mean they will agree. Sometimes they will. Sometimes they will give some very predictable responses. I would bet that, without prompting, you could come up with a list like this one:

- They are too busy. They don't have the time.
- They asked me to do it. It's my job.
- You don't need to see them. I can fill you in. (It's all in the RFP.)
- They don't see consultants (or other lower life-forms).
- It wouldn't be fair to others. We need to keep a level playing field.
- It's not allowed. It's against our policy.
- Put your questions in writing. (We'll share the answers with everyone.)

You could add a couple to the list, and the list would still be rather finite and rather predictable. Chances are they will say something like what is listed here. If the list is finite and predictable, we should be able to think through some intelligent replies that could move us from dysfunctional to functional.

Remember, intent counts more than technique. Our intent is to get a solution that exactly meets their needs. We are only going to pursue two lines of inquiry when we meet with the person we're trying to see: we need to know (1) the *issues* from their perspective, and (2) their *criteria* for making the decision. We are only asking for 20 to 30 minutes with each of them, and are willing to do it over the phone. They only invest 20 to 30 minutes, and you'll invest most of the time.

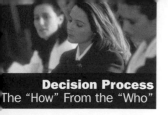

## Match and Lead

If you can't meet
somebody where they
are, you haven't the right
or ability to lead them
somewhere else.

There is a communication tool called "match and lead" which is founded on the idea that if you can't meet somebody where they are, you haven't the right or ability to lead them somewhere else. Milton Erickson, a psychologist, was a master at this method. He was to conversational hypnosis what Steven Hawking is to physics—both confined to wheelchairs and both brilliant at their craft. Erickson started with whatever was presented by clients. He never resisted or tried to change their starting point. He matched them where they were before he offered choices of where to go next. For example, if someone said, "You can't hypnotize me!" he might say, "You're right. There is no way I could hypnotize you! There is no way you could fall, gently, into a light, relaxing, trance." With his voice getting softer he might continue, "There is no way you could begin to relax, to soften your focus; to ease your mind, relaxing, in your own comfortable way, gently…." Before you knew it, people were in a state that they said there was no way they could possibly be in.

Although we may not be Milton Ericksons, as professional communicators, we can use the basics of match and lead. We can truly get on the same side of the table as our counterparts. We can understand where they are coming from. We may have been in the same position ourselves. While we may not agree with them, we can understand them and respect the reasons for their position.

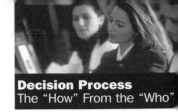
Here is an example:

Gatekeeper:    "They are too busy. You can't see them."

## Match

Consultant:    "I understand they are busy. Particularly with all that's going on. I know my schedule is tight as well. Is it safe to assume that if they are busy, they don't want us to waste their time?"

Gatekeeper:    "Yes."

## Lead

Consultant:    "And that's my concern. In my experience, the biggest waste of their time is when we get them all in a room together and then make a presentation that isn't really relevant and doesn't really address their concerns. They hate that. So let's not waste their time. Let me spend about 20 minutes with each one of them individually, on the phone, before the meeting so we can make the best use of their time during the meeting. You know your company better than I do. How can we set that up?"

Here's another example:

They may say, "It's not fair for you to see them. If we let you do it, we have to do it for everybody." Now don't try and fix their response, just match it. We can certainly understand their desire to be fair, and we appreciate it because we certainly want to be treated fairly. We

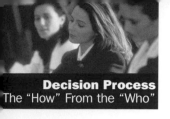
also assume they have a fiduciary responsibility to be fair to the shareholders and stakeholders of their company. And what's fair to them would be a solution that exactly meets their needs. Would it be very fair to produce a solution that exactly met their needs without ever talking to them about those needs? No. And so, in the spirit of fairness, make a suggestion to the client that they only let the vendors talk to those they need to talk to in order to produce the solution that exactly meets their needs. If they don't need to, they won't ask. If we do it that way, that's fair to everybody: it's fair to the client, it's fair to the solution, it's fair to your stakeholders, and it's fair to the other vendors. Out of curiosity, I often ask if anyone else has asked to meet with other people, and the answer is usually no.

## Leaving a "Back Door"

Before you match and lead, it may be helpful to leave a "back door" so if your counterpart refuses your logic, you still have a choice to continue. The decision is ultimately the client's call, and our job is to support their decision. The back door might sound like, "Bill, I know this is your responsibility, and my job is to support you in it. Whatever you decide is what we'll go with. Do you mind if I share some thoughts?" Now you're ready to go for it, and if they shoot you down, you haven't painted yourself into a corner. You can still say, "I appreciate you're at least listening to me. As I said before, my job is to support you. If that's your decision, so be it."

## Intent Counts More Than Technique

Remember that talking to these people is a solution. It won't be convincing to the gatekeeper unless it solves a problem or shows a result. The problem is a solution that doesn't make sense. The result is a proposal that truly addresses the real needs of the company. In the end, they may select someone else, and we understand that. At least the client is going to get our best thinking about how we can help them succeed. Does the thinking sound reasonable? Does it sound reasonable to expect that we could give them a solution that exactly meets their needs by guessing?

Never make a proposal or presentation to people whose criteria for judging you are unknown to you. That is major-league guessing.

## Playing Probabilities

Our choices, and chances, look something like this:

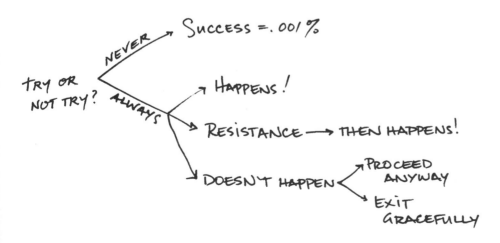

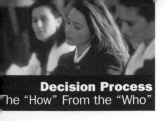
## Are You Ignorant or Arrogant?

I had a client once who was working with a *Fortune 100* company. She needed to see their board of directors to really have a grasp of what their needs were. As she tried to meet with people at such a high level, the main point of resistance was a gatekeeper determined to not give her access. So she said to the gatekeeper, "My company's only goal in this is to get you a solution that exactly meets your needs, and based on what you're telling me, the board of directors are the owners of those needs. To understand what they need, I will need to talk to them." The gatekeeper said, "That can't happen." So she made one move after another to get access, each one met with dogged resistance. There were only three companies proposing, and her company was one of the top companies in this particular area. She said, "I respect your decision to not let me speak to the board. I don't agree with it, I respect it. I hope you'll respect my decision not to propose. This is too important of a project and too high of visibility to make guesses about what they need. I'll end up wasting their time and embarrassing my company. We're either going to end up looking ignorant or arrogant. I'm unwilling to commit my company's name or proposal when I don't even understand what they consider to be important."

The gatekeeper said to her, "If you don't want to propose, then don't propose. That's your choice." She walked away, and had to tell her client manager what she had done. Luckily, her client manager had been through my course and backed her up; otherwise she might

have had some serious problems, because this was a very big deal. She was at home that night (as she tells the story) saying to herself, "What have I done to my career? My family?" Then she received a call from her client manager who said, "I just received a call from one of the directors of (the company). They heard we weren't proposing and asked why. When I told them your reasons, he said that was crazy, and they want to meet with you." She talked to everyone on the board of directors and, after she finished talking to them, they gave her the contract on the spot. They didn't even get the bids from the other two companies. Although that was admittedly a high-risk strategy, she was so committed to a solution that exactly met their needs that she was willing to walk away rather than guess. And when people understood her intent, not only did they invite her in, they gave her the business.

## Choices

If we get blocked, we have some choices:

1. Chunk it down.
2. Go around.
3. Decide not to play.
4. Play anyway.

## Chunk It Down

We don't need to see everyone at once. We only absolutely need to see the people in the step we are about to enter. We may agree in advance that only if we get a green light in the upcoming step will we then talk to the people in succeeding steps.

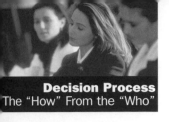

Within a step, we can get permission to see one person at a time. Ask your counterpart if there is one person out of the group of people you want to see with whom he or she feels comfortable (and safe). Ask to see that one person together (or to have your counterpart listen in on the phone conversation). If, and only if, he or she feels the conversation added value will it be extended it to another person. Your counterpart maintains control.

## Go Around

It is clearly a high-risk tactic to go around your counterpart when he or she doesn't want you to. *You* don't have to do it. You can have someone "higher" than yourself talk to the person higher than your counterpart. If the person higher than you is using the same lines of inquiry (issues and criteria), you will get the needed information. And sometimes the risk of not going around is greater than the risk of doing nothing.

## Decide Not to Play

When people are unwilling or unable to give us good information or access to people we need to see, we may decide that this is a fatal flaw in producing a solution that exactly meets their needs. Whether innocently or due to ulterior motives, they make our involvement vulnerable—both in the probability they would select us and that we could produce a workable solution. We may feel that our time could be more productively spent with companies and people who want to interact more effectively. This could be a reason to "offer gracefully to exit."

## Play Anyway

If you left a "back door," you still have the option of proceeding to the Exact Solution step, even though it isn't likely to be exact. Sometimes, if we figure that we have as good a chance of guessing as anyone else, let's roll the dice. Perhaps we'll figure it out after they hire us. At least we are aware of the choice we are making and the risks it incurs.

## What About the Time?

I would rather spend my time talking to human beings than writing a formal guessing document (a proposal). We're not using *more* time in talking to these people, we're using our time *differently*. We're using our time talking human being to human being rather than word processor to word processor. And often when we talk to them, they haven't really thought it through, so we can add value, understand what's important to them, and begin building relationships. The old cliché is, "People don't care how much you know until they know how much you care." And if they don't care to spend 20 minutes, what are they telling you? So let's get real, or let's not play.

## Their Criteria

When you talk to the other people involved in making the decision, you want to find out the issues from their perspective and their criteria for making the decision. To finish our examination of the decision process, let's look at some criteria of interest:

1. The competition (how they will decide between alternative solutions)

**From each person you want to understand:**

1. **ORD from their perspective.**

2. **Their criteria for making the decision.**

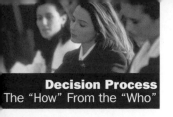

2. Gain/loss (who is perceived to win or lose if the solution is adopted)

3. Personal stake (how they personally stand to win or lose if this thing is adopted)

## External Competition

I am sometimes curious to know who the external competition is. If so, I ask. Some clients find it helpful if you can position what you do versus what others do. What I really want to know is their criteria for choosing among alternative solutions. I am not as concerned about who the competition is as I am about how the client will decide between them. Given they have good companies to choose from, and that all those companies are going to say roughly the same thing (we have really good people, we've done good things for others like you, we'll do good things for you), how is the client going to figure out which one's really the best? We want to know the differences that make a difference.

We often must be patient. We must be skillful at "peeling the onion." They may not have thought out their reasons, which means no one else has had access to their beliefs. We can add value in helping to articulate those beliefs and simultaneously be better able to position our strengths against their criteria.

If they won't tell us, it may be for some very good reasons. We can say, "Fair enough. If you aren't willing to share your thoughts, it's probably for some very good reasons. Could you at least share some of the reasons?" Perhaps they don't have any good reasons, nor do

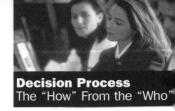

they even care. That is also important information. If they say, "Why do you need to know?" then we share our intent—to get a solution that exactly meets their needs.

## The Incumbent

If they've been working with an incumbent, and they're asking you to bid, what's the concern in your mind? Is this just a market check or price check, or is this a real opportunity? What is the client's motivation to change? Usually, there is a transition cost associated with change. Just like professional boxing, you can't be equal to the incumbent, you have to be demonstrably better. What would be so compelling a difference that they would actually kick out an incumbent?

## Do-It-Yourselfers

I often hear from consultants that two of their biggest competitors are "doing nothing" or "doing it themselves." There is always internal competition because there are always competing uses for resources. And if they really feel they can do it themselves, perhaps that's their best option. Let's get real. If these are options, talk about it. Examples:

- "Is doing nothing an option?"
- "Are there competing uses of funds that might take precedence over this project?"
- "I get the sense that one viable option would be to do this yourselves. Have you given that thought?"

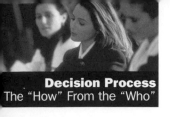
If any answers are yes, we want to know, "What would it take to drive your decision *one way or the other?*" In other words, what are their criteria for this decision?

## Who Stands to Win/Lose?

In today's corporate world, the introduction of any solution, particularly with outside people, may cause some people to feel they won or lost. People who perceive themselves as benefiting could potentially champion our cause. People who perceive they are losing may try to sabotage the deal. We will never know unless we ask.

We could say something like:

- "Clearly, the solution will help the organization. Yet, in thinking about all the people affected, is there anyone who stands to lose?"
- "Who might be perceived to win or lose if this solution is adopted?"
- "This project seems to make a lot of sense for the organization as a whole. Is there anyone who would have a vested interest in the project not happening?"
- "How important is it to you *personally* that this project be successful?" (On a scale of 1 to 10…)
- "What do you personally win or lose as a result of this project?"

If we find out there are people who perceive themselves at a disadvantage, we have some choices. We can talk to them and find out if there is a way to understand and meet their needs. Or if they are

unwilling to honestly explore, we can ask our sponsors for ways to mitigate their impact.

## In the Best Interest of Whom?

People may make decisions in their own best interest, not necessarily in the organization's best interest. If we can understand how they personally stand to win or lose, we have a chance to align what's in their best interest with what's in the organization's best interest. Fortunately, and increasingly, an individual can't win unless he or she does something that makes the organization win. There's so much pressure in the competitive global market that if you're not producing results that make the corporation better, then you're in trouble. Nonetheless, there are also conflicting rewards and goals within an organization. In a complex entity, this is almost nonoptional. If you can find out the metrics of their success (how they personally get rewarded), and tie the metrics of your solution to their metrics as individuals, then the possibility of having your solution perceived as being good goes up. You may even have the opportunity to have your solution resolve conflicting objectives, thus providing additional value.

## In Conclusion

In a complex opportunity, we need to discuss ORD with many people. They will have different perspectives on *Opportunity*—issues, evidence, impact, context, and constraints. They may have differing opinions and knowledge about *Resources*—time, people, and money. They may have a different understanding of the *Decision Process*— the

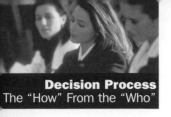

decisions, and who gets involved. They may have differing criteria for the decision. Let's find out. The better we understand the situation, the more likely we are to produce a solution that makes sense, is implemented, and succeeds.

# 23
# The Exact Solution

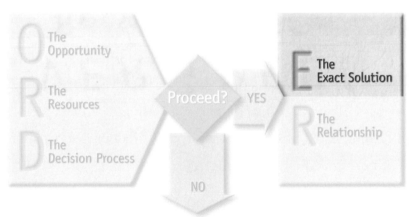

## A Key Transition

The separation of ORD from ER marks the transition from inquiry
(seeking first to understand) to advocacy (seeking to be understood).
As professional communicators, we need to be highly skilled at both.
The better job we do of inquiry, the more powerfully we can advocate
our ability to help the client succeed.

If we have done a good job in ORD, we have a viable opportunity worth pursuing, sufficient resources to make that opportunity a reality, a decision process that is mutually understood and agreed on, and access to the key people we need to see. It may not be perfect (it never is); at least it seems reasonable. If so, we proceed to developing and presenting an exact solution. If not, we either exit gracefully or, if we play anyway, allocate resources more conservatively.

The more clients are willing to cooperate, the more value we can produce for them. Even if they don't select us, they get our best thinking and a more compelling choice. We, of course, need to earn that cooperation through good communication skills (EQ) and critical thinking (IQ). It is a great irony when clients somehow think it is in their best interest to withhold information, deny access, or make us tell, accept, or guess. Assuming we are intelligent business people (do they want to hire stupid business people?), they are telling us to give them less of our time, thought, and energy.

## Proposals Don't Sell—People Do

Proposals don't do the work; they don't help people succeed—it's human beings. Why go through all the effort to talk extensively to several people and then relegate our findings to pieces of paper? Proposals are horrible business-development vehicles. They can be adequate to confirm what's already been agreed to, and if you are counting on a written document to do your advocacy for you, you are in bad shape.

The bad news about formal proposals is that most are poorly com-
posed, are poorly written, include a lot of unneeded information, are
hard to comprehend, and are usually much too long. The good news
is nobody reads them anyway. One study showed that decision makers spend about five minutes per proposal. What will they look at in
five minutes? The price and some overview of what you want to say.
What do we have in person that we lack in writing?

*Vocal cues.* We can hear the tone, emphasis, inflection, and pace of
language. Have you ever sent an e-mail or letter that you thought was
very funny (it sounded funny when you said it to yourself), but was
dead on arrival?

*Visual cues.* We get powerful nonverbal feedback.

*Interaction.* There is give and take; we can respond to questions,
address concerns, and react.

*Flexibility.* If something is not working, we can change; we can react
to new developments, challenges, and directions. How valuable!

*Rapport.* People feel who we are as human beings and vice versa.

*Mutual understanding.* It's hard to come to a true meeting of the minds
in a written document and without some of the factors on this list.

*Closure.* We have the opportunity to conclude, to know what it would
take, or to know that we can't.

Why would we—or the client—ever give up these benefits unless it
were very impractical? It usually happens like this: The client says,
"Send me a proposal," and we say, "O.K." It's what we are used to
doing. We can do better.

## Never Present in Writing What You Could Present in Person

We desire a meeting where we can present our findings in a "What if..." oral presentation: "If we did this, would it be a solution that meets your needs? If not, where does it have to change?" The general thought process for suggesting an in-person meeting is:

1. I think we have a good understanding of what you would like to accomplish, what resources are available, and how you'd like to make this decision.

2. What I would like to do now is:

   - Meet with my team.

   - Develop our best thinking on a solution that exactly meets your needs.

   - Have my team meet with your team.

   - Have you challenge our best thinking with your best thinking.

3. I'm confident of two things:

   a. You're going to be very excited about some of the things we come up with.

   b. Something will be missing or not quite right. The only way we will know what's off is by meeting face to face.

4. After that meeting, we'll write up our findings into a formal document, give it to you, and you can make whatever decision is in the best interest of your company. Does that sound reasonable?

## Yes or No?

If we are the only company involved, gaining agreement shouldn't be a problem. Even if it is competitive, some will agree. With others, we can expect some predictable push-backs:

- We don't have the time.
- It wouldn't be fair.
- If we let you do it, we would have to let everyone do it.
- Why can't you just send the proposal?

Remember our intent? We want a solution that exactly meets their needs. Remember what we have in person that we don't have in writing? (See above.) Neither the client nor we should compromise at this point. Allow me to make a slight diversion, and then we'll come back and look at how we might respond.

## Equivalence of Action

Looking back on successful projects and purchases, most clients cite good partnerships and trusting relationships as paramount. Partners engage in reciprocity, in quid pro quo; they share actions; they work together; they make joint decisions and keep each other informed. Yet in trying to select a trusted partner, the buying process often makes partnering and trust prohibitive. We are looking for equivalence of action. The prospective client is asking us to spend a large amount of our company's resources to prepare a solution that will truly meet their needs. *All we are asking for is the right to present that solution in person.* We spend, perhaps, tens to hundreds of person hours prepar-

ing the solution, and we only ask for a couple hours of their time to present it. Isn't that a reasonable exchange of energy? Isn't that fair? Wouldn't the client appreciate the same opportunity if they were the sellers rather than the buyers? If the development and presentation of a solution has value to the client, they should be willing to exchange value in terms of time or money.

I knew of two companies both proposing on a very large deal. Both estimated they spent a minimum of $250,000 preparing the proposal. At least seven companies were involved. No one was allowed to talk to the people most involved in the project. All presentations were in writing. At the end, they even had to remove the name of their company so the reviewers wouldn't be biased. No one was awarded the project. Isn't there something wrong with this picture?

## Homogeneity Does Not Equal Good Decision Making

Where is it written that by keeping everyone "equal," companies make better decisions? The federal government has strict rules on trying to keep everyone "equal" to keep out corruption and promote fair play. From a governmental purchasing perspective, the goal isn't to get the best solution—it's to obey the law. Whether you agree with the process or not, would you say the government is a model of purchasing efficiency and effectiveness to be emulated by the business world?

Does "leveling the playing field" make for better decisions? It doesn't seem so. Purchasing is not television programming where we are try-

ing to address the lowest common denominator. As a buyer of goods and services, I would like competing alternatives to clearly differentiate themselves and make the best possible case for how they can help me. How do I gain by removing differentiation and creativity and trying to make everyone be alike? Since people (not pieces of paper) deliver the solution, why would I eliminate direct interaction with people from my consideration? Do I really feel people are interchangeable parts—a commodity? If I believe "commoditizing" the process brings me a lower price, I am fine if I am buying a true commodity. I might be horribly misguided and shortchanged if I'm *not* dealing with a commodity.

Dysfunctional buying practices have arisen to combat dysfunctional selling practices. Buyers don't want to be abused by manipulation or have their time wasted by incompetence. A less effective solution may be more preferable than talking to a lot of people who want you to do what's good for them rather than what's good for you. Even if you really like them, it makes it harder to tell them no. So you keep a "level playing field" where you won't have to talk to *anybody*.

## When the Rules Don't Work...

Our rule is, "When the rules are dysfunctional, break the rules," including this one.

**Time.** Clients often say they don't have time for a two-hour presentation, yet they can spend years living with or trying to correct a solution that doesn't meet their needs. If time is the real issue, spending

time up front makes the most sense. Also, we have to spend a lot of time preparing the solution, and we are only asking for a little time to present it.

**Fairness 1.** Be fair to a solution that best meets the client's needs. Let each provider present in the way that makes the most sense to them. If they want to present in person, they will ask. If they are content to respond in writing, that's fine. Let each do what they think best reflects them and their solution. Let the buyer decide.

**Fairness 2.** Fairness should be two-way. They are asking us to commit a large amount of resources to prepare the solution (with no guarantee of adoption), and we are asking for relatively little time to present it in person. To do otherwise doesn't seem fair. Reciprocity, quid pro quo, and equivalence of action are fair.

**Level playing field.** Homogeneity does not make for optimal decisions unless it is a true commodity.

**Why not send a proposal?** Written communication is less rich than in-person communication. It's not the best for either party. We'll bring a proposal, we'll just present it in person.

When I ask to present in person, and the client says they are getting written proposals from the other companies, I usually say something like, "Great. Please get their proposals, read them thoroughly, and when we sit down to talk, you'll have better information to work with."

**Exact Solution**

## If They Insist

Try as we might, the client may insist on a written proposal. Perhaps it is a screening device to reduce many companies to a few. Perhaps it is their "policy," and it's not open to examination. If that's the case, then:

1. Try to gain agreement for an in-person "pre-proposal meeting," a "trial run," a "draft session," with one or more key stakeholders to test out your thinking. If granted, follow the "What if…" oral presentation guidelines. If they ask why, our answer is this: *"It is to no one's advantage to put ideas or concepts in the final written proposal if they don't make sense to the client."*

2. Failing that, try for a telephone review of the key elements with one or more key stakeholders—for the same reasons as above.

3. *Gain agreement to present your formal written proposal in person.* I said present…not just deliver. The reason? Equivalency of action. You will spend a lot of time writing the proposal; you ask for only a little time to present it in person. *Only if all else fails will I send a formal written proposal in the mail with no human interaction.* This is a major yellow light. Optimal decisions happen human being to human being, not word processor to word processor.

## Writing Is Not Bad!

I am not saying writing is bad. We will work hard to craft a discussion outline and probably some slides for our presentation. An engagement letter that confirms what we have agreed to in person is superb. When we write a proposal, we should apply excellent writing skills. I'm just saying that proposals don't sell—people do.

> **It is to no one's advantage to put ideas or concepts in the final written proposal if they don't make sense to the client.**

> **Only if all else fails, send a formal written proposal in the mail with no human interaction.**

## The Purpose of the Presentation

Your presentation should:

- Give evidence and proof that you can solve the client's problems and/or achieve their desired results.
- Fit their available resources.
- Match their decision criteria.
- Enable the client to decide.

At this point, you should feel confident of the above. If not, any yellow lights were tested along the way and didn't turn to red.

## Keep the End in Mind

Before *every* interaction with the client, we should ask ourselves, "What is appropriate for them to *say, do,* or *decide* at the end of this interaction?" If this is a sole source presentation, what is reasonable to expect? That they will do this with us or they won't. If it is a competitive situation, what is reasonable? Probably *not* a final decision to go or not go with us. It does seem reasonable they could decide if this is or isn't a solution that exactly meets their needs, and if not, what has to change? Our presentation should be organized to allow those decisions, with confidence.

## Keep Your Presentations Interactive

A colleague and I walked into a finalist presentation meeting not too long ago. The client had prepared for the typical two-hour presentation. The first thing I said when we walked in was, "I think we may

have a problem. You've invited us here for a two-hour dog-and-pony show, and if you hire us, we're going to tell your people to never do that. It's not effective! So it would be kind of funny for us to stand up here and do something we will teach you never to do. Let me ask: Would it be all right with you if we just talked this through, to see what makes sense and what doesn't make sense?" This client had just endured many hours of slide presentations in a darkened room and had been presented "at." They were very appreciative of the opportunity for dialogue. It made a huge difference. (Of course, the only reason we could use this approach is that we had taken the time to talk to all of these people individually, and felt extremely prepared to talk about their relevant and important issues.)

So when I say "present," I'm not talking about the 184 PowerPoint® slides with four of your people presenting 20 minutes a piece. I'm also not talking about a casual, unprepared conversation. I am talking about series of modules, each of which includes some presentation and some discussion, followed by a decision.

Many presentations are structured with a given amount of presentation followed by a stipulated time for Q&A. Yet, would you say most presentations are usually longer or shorter than the allotted time? And do presentations start on time? What part of the presentation usually gets cut short? The Q&A! If so, we are losing a vital part of what makes presenting in person so powerful—the human interaction. Below is a format I have found effective.

## Presentation Format

This is only one of many ways to present. It is consistent with the ORDER approach. I use this sequence often. I also modify it often to fit the circumstances. You may add, modify, or delete to meet your needs.

1. *Thank them for the time they have invested to this point.* Let them know it was extremely helpful in developing your ideas.
2. *Suggest mutual self-interests.* "We have mutual self-interests. It's win-win if we get it, and lose-lose if we don't. We both want a solution that truly meets your needs."
3. *State the objective for the presentation.* "Our objective today is to find out: *Is this a solution that meets your needs? If not, what would have to change?* We understand you may find a better solution, in which case you'll purchase it. Our goal is to get your explicit feedback today on whether this solution would work. Is that fair to expect?"
4. *Review organizational context.* "Here is our understanding of the big picture…" If appropriate, discuss it mutually.
5. *Review problem evidence and impact* (current-state). Ask them to make sure you got it right and that you didn't leave anything out. Let them add, modify, or delete.
6. *Review result evidence and impact* (future-state). Discuss. Let them add, modify, or delete.
7. *Review selection criteria.* Discuss. Let them add, modify, or delete. Note: At this point you should have accomplished the following:
   - Demonstrated a tremendous understanding of the client and their business. If there are multiple decision makers, you are

often the only person in the room who has talked with each individual.

- Obtained collective buy-in to the pain of the present state, the gain of the future state, and the criteria for the decision. Time has passed. Things change. This may be one of the few times the decision makers have met together. It is important to gain consensus on motivation and criteria.

8. *Propose your solution including fees.*

   a. "You said your primary issue is X. Here is what we would do. Here is proof we know how to do it. Here is how we would meet your criteria. What's your sense—could you check this issue off, or is something missing?"

   b. "You said your next issue is Y…" Same process.

   c. Continue checking off issues in priority.

   d. Present timing, division of labor, and fees.

9. *Enable a decision*

   When you are two-thirds of the way through the presentation, whether you have finished all the issues or not, take time out to see where you are. Ask, "Based on what you've seen and heard so far, is this a solution that, for all intents and purposes, meets your needs?" (If not, what would have to change?)

## Enable a Decision

Not deciding is a decision, and often a suboptimal one. Often consultants get to the end of a presentation and nothing happens. The client may be effusive with praise, thank us for our time, ask us to do some additional actions—yet no decision is made. We gained the

**Exact Solution**

client's agreement at the beginning of the presentation that they would *explicitly* answer the questions: "Is this a solution that for all intents and purposes, meets your needs? If not, what would have to change?" We are not asking them to buy, or to even commit to us. We *are* asking that they state, out loud, what they think, feel, and believe to be true at that moment. We are not asking for their *final* decision—we are asking them to decide on the viability of what we presented.

You can ask them to discuss their beliefs individually or to talk about them as a group. You can allow the comments to be free-form. You can calibrate by asking them to state where they are on a scale of 1 to 10—where 10 is a solution that meets their needs (nothing is perfect), and 1 is completely missing the boat. You can ask them to literally or metaphorically hold up a green, red, or yellow light. You can use anonymous electronic voting. However you do it, *you must facilitate authenticity about what they believe* as closely as possible. Those beliefs can appear when you are present and can interact with them, or they can appear when you have left and have no influence.

## Resolving Concerns

What happens if there is a yellow light, a "5," or a stated concern? Research on "objections" shows that many are simply a lack of accurate information. If concerns are stated, we can provide the missing information. Others are true challenges to our approach, abilities, and experience, or perhaps the relative merits of our solution vs. the competing choices. This topic is worth a small book in itself. Here are some ideas:

The key to answering a concern is to find out the real concern! Often the question they ask is not the real question. Listen thoroughly to what the concern is (and check your ego at the door). Ask enough questions to truly understand rather than guess. If you guess, you will likely guess your worst fear. Their concern is often less challenging than your worst fear.

A good friend of mine—now a great sales trainer—used to be a salesperson for a computer company I owned. He had worked on a large sale for about six months, and was making his final presentation to the CEO and key decision makers. At the end of his presentation, about which everyone seemed enthusiastic, the CEO asked him, "I like what you've shown us. How big is your company?" My friend's worst fear was that this large company would think we were too small to execute and support such a large installation. He proceeded to make every statement he could conjure up that would make us seem big. The CEO listened patiently, then said, "Gosh, sounds like you're pretty big. That's too bad. We are committed to work with a small company who will give us the best service possible. We just worked with (a large computer company) and they ignored us. We won't make the same mistake again. But thank you for coming out to visit us."

The question wasn't "How big is your company?" It was "Will you give us good service?" If my friend had asked, "We are (dollars revenue, number of employees)—is the size of the company important to your decision?" or, "I'd be glad to describe the size of our com-

pany—I sense you're asking for a reason. Could you share the reason?" or if he would have allowed the CEO to talk more about what was on his mind, he could have addressed the real question. He now sometimes states, "The question they ask you is *never* the real question!" Perhaps he is just stressing the point.

We can't get real until we find out what we are really dealing with. Often clients use high-level abstractions to signal their concerns ("open systems," "scalable solutions," "local presence," "global presence," "appropriate experience," etc.). If we perceive this as either a weakness or strength, we may plunge in and answer the wrong question.

## What Would Have to Happen...?

**"What would have to happen to resolve that concern to your complete satisfaction?"**

If the client has a concern, state the concern accurately (from the client's perspective). If appropriate, "match." For example, "I can appreciate your position. If I felt that way, I'd have a concern too." *"What would have to happen to resolve that concern to your complete satisfaction?"* Amazingly, they often have less demanding criteria than you. And if you address their concerns in terms of their criteria, it is usually much more convincing.

## How Do *They* Solve It?

The client has to sell their products and services. What do they say to their customers to resolve similar concerns? For instance, let's say we are entering a new market niche and the client challenges us on our experience in that niche. We could ask, "Your company has successfully entered several new market niches. When you were convinced

Exact Solution

that you had a truly superior solution for your prospective client, and the client challenged your direct experience in that niche, what did you say?" Clearly, we will listen closely to the response as a cue for what we might say as well. Of course, we could also just give them our response directly, without getting those cues.

## Analogy

We can sometimes create an analogy between our methods of business and theirs. I was working on a large computer-system opportunity with the owner of a chain of retail shoe stores. He liked our system, and yet thought other systems had the same look and feel, and were less expensive. His stores sold premier-brand shoes. I asked him his reason for selling premier brands rather than "knock-offs"; the latter were cheaper and had larger margins. He said, "Those other shoes may look similar on display, and when our customers wear them daily, they quickly look shoddy and are not at all as comfortable. We get more returns and fewer satisfied customers. And our business is about satisfied customers." Can you imagine the analogy I made to our computer systems?

## Metaphors and Stories

Metaphors and stories are powerful communication tools. Just think of spiritual leaders and other effective teachers. A metaphor is a way of speaking about one thing in terms of another, hopefully bringing new insight to the topic of consideration. Metaphors that resolve concerns retain the same structure and nature of the client's problematic situation, talk about it in another context, and provide a solution. The classic "third-person story" is a metaphor. Rather than give

direct logic, we tell our client how another client had the same concern, analyzed it, and satisfied it to their complete satisfaction (and perhaps surprise).

We might embed a metaphor or story. For instance, perhaps executive team members are suggesting that "everyone else" in the company go through leadership training, and are putting off attending the training themselves because of more pressing "fires." We might say something like, "I completely understand. Our company was doing the same thing. We're very good at reacting to sudden threats and crises, and we were very poor at recognizing the need to invest in learning and development. Our CEO was on the airplane the other day and actually listened to the flight attendant's instructions. (I usually don't.) I was reminded that in case of an emergency, and the oxygen mask drops down, to first place it on myself and then on my children. As I talk to various companies, I wonder, how often we ask others to do something that we are not willing to do ourselves, and it ends up not helping anyone?"

## Direct Logic

We can offer straightforward logic to address a concern or to prove a point. Our logic will be more compelling if it is offered in the language or mental models of the client.

## Predictable Concerns

My goal here is not to demonstrate or discuss how to resolve all concerns, objections, and stalls (though I would love to write a book on

that topic). I will say they are finite and largely predictable. That means we can take some time and think through the communication and business-logic challenges they present. We don't have to struggle every time they come up. We can create compelling analogies, metaphors, stories, and rationale. We can calmly ask questions and uncover the real concern knowing we have a well-thought-out response or approach once we find it. We can ask them, "What would have to happen?" confident their criteria is often less strenuous than ours.

One of my most enjoyable and stimulating assignments with clients is to work on their predictable objections. In the framework of "getting real," the challenge may be to change the business model rather than come up with a great metaphor. If I am told, "Our competitor is selling the exact same product at a significantly lower price. How can we overcome that objection?" I usually say, "You can't! If you were a consumer and could buy the exact same product for less money, wouldn't *you* do it? What possible reason would you have for paying more money?" If they can't offer a compelling answer, then there is nothing to talk about.

Often, however, we are dealing with subjective perceptions. For clients (perhaps all of us), perceptions are reality. If you can expand or modify perceptions, reality changes. And when we say, *"Let's get real"*—"real" according to whom? To have a meaningful dialogue, to play on the boundaries of perception, is exciting and intellectually stimulating.

## Price Concerns

One predictable statement is, "Your price is too high." Linguists call this a "missing comparison." Too high compared to what? Compared to what they were hoping we would say? To what they have in their budget? To what they are authorized to spend? To what our competitors are saying? To nothing—they're just negotiating?

You will receive far less price resistance with the ORDER methodology. You developed considerably more value in the Opportunity than the investment in your solution; otherwise it was a yellow light. You already tested out a price range in Resources. You developed relationships, rapport, and understanding as you talked to people in the Decision Process. I've had clients tell me, "Be sure whatever price you come in at is one you feel good about—we need your head in the game." I've had clients tell me to *raise* my price—in one instance by over a million dollars. (They thought through the total situation more accurately than I had.)

**If clients challenge you on price, don't take it personally!**

However, if clients challenge you on price, *don't take it personally!* So many times all they have to say is a version of "Well, we'd really like to do business with you, but your price is too high," and consultants immediately drop the price, leaving the client to contemplate how stupid or fiscally irresponsible they would have been not to say something. The consultants, of course, try to compensate for their incompetence by raising their prices more so they can afford to give a discount. Many professionals are vulnerable to price challenges

because they:

- Don't establish value up front.
- Know their prices are flexible.
- Believe that all price challenges are real.
- Believe that their counterpart knows competitive pricing.
- Dislike discussing prices.
- Focus on defending prices rather than providing results.
- Want the sale.

Sophisticated buyers of professional services will frequently challenge the quoted prices for the following reasons:

- They lose nothing by challenging the price.
- They feel it is their responsibility.
- Sellers of services often give in on price.
- Value has not been created up front.
- They do not understand what it really takes to provide the solution.

Unsophisticated buyers may feel at risk because they do not understand:

- The time needed to perform a complex service.
- The legitimacy of "high" rates. (They equate rates with salary.)
- The specific deliverables.
- The expected benefits.

## Good Negotiation Won't Compensate for Bad Consulting!

To win at chess, you can't just study the end game. There is no end game unless you've had a good beginning and middle. In baseball, the best "closer" in the world will never get a "save" unless the team gets to the last inning with a lead. If you didn't do a good job in ORD, expect difficulty on price. You are trying to help the client make an ROI decision. The "I" is easy to find—it's on the last page of your proposal. The question is, where is the "R"? If there is no "R," your "I" is a "C"—a cost. And the cost is always too high.

## I'm a Liar and I'm Stupid

**Only deal with price when it's the last issue on the table.**

Assuming you've completed ORD, and you are presenting your solution, then *only deal with price when it's the last issue on the table.* It's painful to observe how many consultants compromise on price and still don't get the business. In effect, they tell the client, "I am a liar (my price is not my price) and I am stupid." And price may not be the real issue. One study showed that for 65 percent of clients who gave price as the primary reason for turning down a vendor, price was, in reality, only a secondary concern. If we discover the primary concern and deal with it, the concern about price might go away, or be greatly mitigated.

If our price is "too high," what is the number the client is thinking of *and how did they come up with that number?* We need to closely examine and understand the answer to that question. If there are issues

other than price, let's talk about them.

In a competitive situation, to find out if price is the last issue on the table, take price off the table and see what happens. "Let's say all your proposals were exactly the same price, what would you do?" If they say, "Clearly, we would go with you," then price is the last issue on the table. We can respond, "I appreciate that. What are some of the reasons that make us a clear-cut choice?" (And don't those reasons substantiate the differential?) We may not compromise on price; at least we know it's the last issue.

**To find out if price is the last issue on the table, take price off the table and see what happens.**

If they hesitate at all, or can't easily decide, then price is *not* the last issue on the table. Something else is going on. Let's get real and find out what it is. I will sometimes say to clients, "Our goal is to get you a solution that exactly meets your needs, and if it's not clear we have the best solution, you shouldn't buy it at any price, even if our price is lower. With price off the table, what's keeping this from being a clear-cut decision?"

## If Price Is the Last Issue

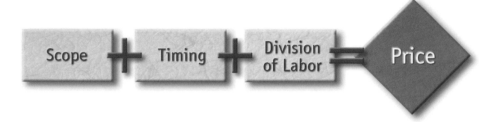

Price is a function of scope (what we are providing), plus timing (how fast we provide it), plus division of labor (who does what).

If price is the last issue, is there a *realistic* trade-off on one of the price equivalents? Can they live with less of a result? Can they accept a longer or shorter time frame (depending on the value of time to you)? Can they handle more of their effort, less of yours? If not, *then that's the price!* That's how we came up with that price.

## Never Give Something for Nothing

Never give the same scope, timing, and division of labor at just a lower price. Never! Please! Unilateral concessions on price only convince the purchaser they were right to beat you up on price, and they always will. Your only recourse is to artificially raise your prices so they can beat you up. You reinforce a dysfunctional practice.

**If you have to give a concession, get a value exchange in return.**

If you have to give a concession, *get a value exchange in return.* It doesn't have to be monetary. Some examples include:

- You don't have to write a formal proposal (only an "engagement letter"), and you pass the savings on to them.

- The client agrees to provide certain marketing and advertising value based on their true experience with your company.

- The client provides some R&D work that can be leveraged on other opportunities—perhaps they commit resources to measuring results.

- They sign up additional business now and get a volume discount.

- They pay early.

Think of *your* company's profit and loss statement. What line on that statement will get charged for *this* discount? How will the client contribute to that line item in return?

## Caveat

I am fully aware I am not offering a complete course in negotiating skills, either on price or on resolving concerns. Let's leave that to another book—mine or somebody else's. These are basic principles and practices that should be helpful.

## What Now?

We have presented our solution. We have resolved, to our best ability, any discrepancies in a "solution that exactly meets their needs." The client will say, "We want to go with you," "We don't want to go with you," or they won't choose. Based on their response, there are some actions to take to ensure a productive and positive ongoing relationship. That is the subject of the next chapter.

**Exact Solution**

# 24
# The Relationship

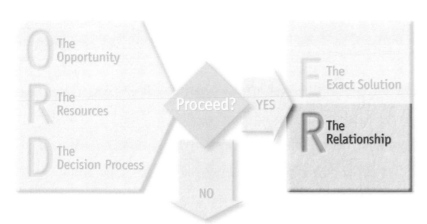

We have presented our "exact" solution, and resolved any concerns or challenges to the best of our ability. The client is likely to react:

> *No, thank you.*
> *No decision.*
> *Yes, let's do it.*

No matter what their response, to successfully complete the ORDER cycle, we need to do some more work to ensure a productive and positive ongoing relationship. Let's look first at "no," then "no decision," then "yes."

## No, Thank You

This is straightforward. I'm not adding intellectual capital here. I am encouraging you to do what is common sense, and not common practice. If they say "No, thank you," we want to:

1. Thank them for their investment of time and energy. (Save any cursing for your own private moments.)

2. Ask where our solution failed to meet their needs, or how some other solution was superior.

This information is so valuable, yet so infrequently obtained. Neither of us wants to "get real" at this point. They always tell us we came in a close second—it was a really hard choice. Nobody ever seems to come in third or worse. It is hard for them to get specific about the reasons. Emotionally, it's difficult to be authentic about people's weak points or deficiencies. There may be political considerations. And it is tough intellectually to articulate the true factors. On our side, we are often lost in woe, our ego is disheveled, and we aren't eager to hear the real reasons we lost.

Consultants who clarify the specific reasons for losing can gain incredible information about how to improve. As the old saying goes, "There is no failure—just more information about how to succeed."

3. Plant the seeds of future collaboration. If they valued our participation, and if we have learned how we can serve them better in
   the future, we can ask to be included in other opportunities. We
   can also suggest that if they *do not* get the results they expected, to
   please call us—we'll be glad to help. Most of us have experience
   with clients who pick another provider, are disappointed, and
   come back to us. Let's make that easy.

## No Decision

One of the great services you can afford clients is to help them make
a good decision in their own best interest. As I mentioned before, a
decision not to make a decision is a decision, and usually a suboptimal one. We only got to the point of developing and presenting a
solution because there was significant impact. Either this solution
makes sense for the client and they are losing out every day they hesitate; or it doesn't make sense, and they should wipe it off the agenda;
or there are issues with greater priority (impact). If this last situation
is the case, let's talk about it.

When I get stuck in the "no decision" loop (and I remember to stay
focused rather than move on to something more compelling), I suggest          **No is okay!**
to the client that we set up a series of steps (see "The Decision
Process"), at the end of which they could say with comfort and confidence one of two things: yes or no. And no is okay! I'm not trying to
force them to say yes, just to make a good decision *one way or the other.*

# Yes, Let's Do It

I said earlier that how you sell is a free sample of how you solve. Let me say now that how you solve creates more sales than how you sell. Our true goal is to help clients succeed. The ability to deliver a solution that truly meets the client's needs develops far more sales than any of our selling activities. Happy clients not only give us more business themselves, they are the essential references for everyone else. The classic error of consultants is to get the business and then move on. They leave behind more business than whatever they move on to.

Studies show that profitability is most affected by account retention, account expansion, and being the primary provider of your services in an account. To ensure that we get the benefits from helping our client succeed over the long term, consider the following:

## 1. Make sure all yellow lights, present or future, are turned to green.

Make sure yellow lights are turned to green while the relationship is strong. If there were any outstanding yellow lights that both we and the client ignored, let's talk about them. In every intervention (products or services), there are driving forces motivating the need for the solution, and restraining forces that would limit success. Both we and the client can predict inhibitors. Let's examine them now and see how we can lessen or eliminate their effect.

Let them get out their inhibition list first, and then talk about them: "So if that happens, what should we do?" or, "How would you like to avoid that?" or, "What would we have to do to make you comfortable about that?"

Then give *our* list. We might talk about change of scope, cost over-runs, their failure to deliver on time, people commitments, unexpected impediments, changes in personnel, missed deadlines, etc. Set up lines of good communication now so if something occurs, we know how to talk about it effectively, and we are not caught up in the emotions and fears of the moment when it actually happens.

Don't get distracted by the old cliché of transactional sales: "Once you make the sale, run out the door." In complex sales, we only truly win when the client succeeds. And success has as much to do with removing the constraints as it does with promoting results.

## 2. Ensure a smooth transition from "sales" to delivery.

Another blinding flash of the obvious. We've invested a lot of time understanding the issues, evidence, impact, context, and constraints. It is critical that we work closely with the implementers of the solution to ensure that what they purchased is what they get. Keep a written record of the information you've collected (see "Client Profile" in Appendix A), and create a formal process for passing it on.

**Relationship**

### 3. Keep managing to desired results.

Maintain the pressure on your company and the client to measure
and achieve results. This is both challenging and incredibly important. Have you ever seen a new executive look at expenditures and
say, "Hey. We've spent a lot of money with XYZ. What do we have to
show for it?" And on the flip side, demonstrating "data points" of success creates internal heroes and proof that what you do works.

### 4. Establish an account-management strategy.

We should always be thinking, "How can I help this client succeed?"
If we retain and magnify that focus, there will be multiple opportunities. How do we pursue those opportunities without pushing ourselves on the client? That is the topic of the next chapter.

212

# 25
# Helping *Current* Clients Succeed

We have won the opportunity to work with a client. What now? We should develop a feverish focus on helping them succeed. Not only should we focus intently on the current projects, services, and products, we should be alert to as many additional means for them to succeed as possible—whether with us or someone else.

The physics of account development apply here: *a client at rest tends to stay at rest unless acted upon by an outside force.* For a given client, if that force is internal or external business pressure, they might come to us. If all we do is wait for clients to come to us, we are reactive rather than proactive agents of success. We need to take opportunities to them. We need to be the outside force that gets them moving. Failure to do so limits our value added. How do we take new opportunities to them without being perceived as trying to "sell" them? Here are two strategies: "pull" and "push."

**A client at rest tends to stay at rest unless acted upon by an outside force.**

## Pull Strategy

The pull strategy is easy, effective, and underused. All we need to do is initiate a meeting with key client stakeholders and "structure a conversation" around what is important to them. We might say, "The marketplace, our leadership, and our clients are all pushing us to ensure that our solutions are directly linked to business results. Is that the case with you as well? Could we set up a meeting to fully understand your key priorities for the next 12 months so we can more closely relate everything we do to what matters most to the company?" Those priorities could be strategic or tactical, depending on with whom we are working and the nature of what we provide.

When you have that meeting, you know what to do. Even though *we* called the meeting, we start out on *their* agenda. What are the key issues? What is the evidence, impact, and context? What are the constraints? If the impact is big, would they be interested in thoughts of how to address the issues? Would they collaborate with us to build a business case for the opportunity so we could attract resources and develop a decision process? Are they interested in seeing what an exact solution might look like?

**If you don't treat current clients like new clients, they will become former clients.**

## Who's Talking to Your Clients?

*If you don't treat current clients like new clients, they will become former clients.* Someone else will be talking to them about what's important. Since we have access to our client, and hopefully a good track record of helping them succeed, it should be far easier for us to get a pull meet-

ing than it would be for a stranger. No specific reason is needed to ini-
tiate a pull meeting. Here are some triggering opportunities:

- **Organizational change.** Reorganization, merger, acquisition,
  major market shifts, new products—what are the new priorities?

- **New position/promotion.** New people in new roles—what is
  leadership counting on them to produce?

- **End of an engagement.** Does the client have everything needed
  to carry on? What else is a priority?

- **Project-related milestones.** As you review the progress of a current project, you can scan for other related priorities.

- **Annual, semi-annual, quarterly account strategy sessions.**
  Build into the relationship up front that you will meet periodically
  (no charge) to monitor the relationship and to stay current with
  key priorities.

What would you add?

## Push Strategy

The push strategy begins when we believe one of our products or
services would truly help our client succeed. We'd like to explore
with them the viability of our belief. We'd like them to feel served,
not severed, by our approach. Here is one method. It requires more
homework on our part, yet we end up in front of the client better
prepared and with little downside.

## What We Have

The good news with a current client is we likely have relationships and accessibility. There are people who know us, like us, and are willing to work with us. We have knowledge of the client's business, and as a result, are probably aware of problems they'd like to eliminate or results they would like to achieve.

## What We Lack

What we lack is recognition on their part of a need. They are a body at rest. There is no felt (O)pportunity, so there are no allocated (R)esources, and there is no (D)ecision Process. Other than that, we're in great shape. After all, we have an (E)xact Solution. Typically, we will go to them and explain all the great features and benefits of our exciting solution, and we are amazed when the client doesn't sing hosannas. Or after some initial enthusiasm, nothing happens. If we think they should be moving, and they are content to stay at rest, then:

- They lack evidence of a substantial problem or result.
  (no recognition)
- They have evidence, and they don't see the impact.
  (no motivation)
- They have evidence and impact; they don't see a solution.
  (no hope)
- They have evidence, impact, and a solution, and experience constraints. (no chance)
- They have evidence, impact, a solution, and lack constraints, and have other issues of a higher priority. (no urgency)

## Stimulate and Collaborate

Our first goal is to see if the client is motivated to move. If they lack
evidence of a problem/result, we can stimulate with evidence. If they
lack impact, we can demonstrate it. If they didn't know there was a
possible solution, we can enlighten them. If constraints exist, we can
bring new ways to deal with them. If they have issues of a higher priority, what are they and how can we help? The ORDER process still
applies. The difference is that *we* have to supply a lot of the thinking
in advance. If they see a reason to move, they can *collaborate* with us
to build a business case for the opportunity to which we can attract
resources and develop a decision process. Then we can present an
exact solution, get a decision, and continue the relationship.

## Push Strategy Preparation

For the push strategy, we need to reverse-engineer the opportunity.
Try this out. Pick a specific client for whom you have a solution that
would really make a difference. Follow this procedure:

1. Write down all the problems the organization could experience
   before the solution would be compelling, and/or all the results they
   would have to desire. Stay in the brainstorming mode—no right or
   wrong, good or bad. Write down everything you can think of.

2. For each problem or result you wrote down, what evidence exists
   that the client had the problem or would get the result? Is there
   hard evidence somewhere in the organization? Could you get soft
   evidence by talking to several people? Is there presumed evidence
   from third-party sources? Push yourself to answer the question,

"How could I prove there is a problem or that they would achieve this result?" Then write down where you might get the evidence.

3. For each problem or result (assuming you have proved its existence), what would be the potential impact—financial and otherwise—to the organization if they had the problem or if they achieved the result? Think it through carefully and completely.

4. Who would be most interested in solving the problem or achieving the result?

Here's an example. To complete a worksheet for one of your proposed solutions, see Appendix B.

Account Development Worksheet

Account Development Worksheet

SAMPLE

**Client:**

**Proposed Solution:**

| Problem/Result | Evidence — Type (Hard/Soft, Preferred) | Evidence — Source (What, Where, Who) | Impact | Constraints | People Who Care |
|---|---|---|---|---|---|
| Too little revenue or revenue growth; too little margins; too high cost of sales. | H, P | Plan vs. actual; actual vs. industry/competition | Lower earnings, lower stock price and market evaluations; lower working capital, cash flow; less funding for new or improved products/services; lower rewards for top performers (more T.O.? harder to hire?); potential downward spiral | Company specific | Company specific |
| Too little repeat business | H, P | Percentage of new business from current accounts | May lose accounts because we aren't meeting more of their needs (lower sales); may lose opportunities for getting business at lower costs and possibly higher margins. If we don't meet client's multiple needs, someone else will—if they cross-sell, we may lose the business we have (lower sales). | | |
| Too little follow-on business | H, P | Percentage and dollar amount of sales from add-ons | Lost opportunities for revenue with low cost of sales and potentially higher margins. Someone else gets a foot in the door. | | |
| Too few new opportunities | H, S | Too low ratio from suspects to potential market; too few leads; too few new accounts | Low market share. | | |
| Poor sales efficiency | H, S | Poor ratio of suspects to prospects | Small "pipeline"; lower revenues; higher cost of sales. | | |
| Poor sales effectiveness | H, S | Too low ratio of prospects to close | Lower revenues; higher cost of sales | | |
| Too little penetration of target accounts | H | Target accounts acquired/total target accounts | Lower market share. | | |
| Not getting type of business we want/need | S, P | Percentage of sales in new niches, markets, products, services | Curtails future growth and probably cramps margins; may hurt market perception | | |
| No consistent sales methodology | S | Each person has own method; no explicit model supported by the company. | Less shared knowledge, coaching, strategizing. Lower sales, higher cost of sales. | | |
| Improving average or below average performance | S | So specific metrics. Measures are total performance, not behaviors. | Keep average performers longer; higher management costs; lower revenue per salesperson, higher cost of sales. | | |
| Decreased client loyalty | S | All work put out to bid each year. | Higher cost of sales, lower margins. | | |
| Fleeting competitive advantages | H, S | Competition offers similar products/services in short time frame. | Lower margins. | | |
| Predictable changes in future likely to be disruptive | S | Anecdotal | Sales "hit the wall." | | |

## Example

Solution = Sales Training and Sales Management

Question: What problems would indicate that sales training and/or sales management is a compelling solution?

**Helping *Current*
Clients Succeed**

Account Development Worksheet

SAMPLE

**Proposed Solution:** _____

| Impact | Constraints | People Who Care |
|---|---|---|
| Lower revenues and profit per salesperson. What you can't measure you can't improve. Prohibits ability to "train to a number." Limits coaching effectiveness. Can tell people to get better but can't tell them how. | Company specific | Company specific |
| Hire too few or too many people; don't match supply with demand = missed sales or increased inventory. | | |
| Wasted training dollars; absence and desired results (higher sales and margins, lower costs, etc.); greater cynicism regarding future training. | | |
| Higher costs; lower sales; potentially higher T.O. | | |
| Don't build on success; reinvent the wheel; higher costs; lower costs. | | |
| | | |
| | | |
| | | |

Account Development Worksheet

**Client:** _____

SAMPLE

| Problem/Result | Evidence | | |
|---|---|---|---|
| | Type (H=Hard S=Soft P=Presumed) | Source (What, Where, Who) | |
| No and/or inadequate sales metrics | S | No specific metrics; metrics only measure total performances, no specific behaviors | |
| Poor sales forecasts | H | Wide discrepancy between forecast and actual | |
| Low ROI from training | S, P | No measures. No correlation between sales training and success; low perceived value | |
| Poor allocation of resources between high/low prob. opportunities | S, P | High sales cost; no "sales probability" tools; low proposal to close | |
| Lack of knowledge sharing | S | No consistent way to share what is/isn't working. | |
| | | | |
| | | | |
| | | | |

## Push Strategy Execution

Our goal is to move from the *people we know to the people who care to the people who decide.* Sometimes these are all one person, or one group of people. In a complex proposition and/or organization they may be different. If they are different, this is our flow:

**People we know.** From people who know us, and hopefully respect our work, we want two things: information and introduction. They can guide us to get the evidence and impact data that would confirm a need or objective. They may be able to introduce us to the people who care—the people motivated to solve the problems or achieve the results.

**People who care.** These people are the ones in the last column of the worksheet above. Based on our research and guidance from the people we know, these are the people most motivated to "move." We want to stimulate their interest and get them to *collaborate* in building ORD.

**People who decide.** By the time we reach these people, we should have a sound business case for the adoption of a solution. It should be easy and quick for these people to make a good decision. If we have done good work, the only (logical) reason they should have for saying no is that there are higher priorities. If so, what are they and how can we help?

If the above three categories are all one person or function, we should make clear our process. We have an idea that we believe would really make a difference. We are willing to do a little homework to support

our hypothesis. If, and only if, there is a problem worth solving or a result worth obtaining will we engage them around a solution.

## To Move or Not to Move, That Is the Question

Since intent counts more than technique, hopefully the reason we are trying to get the client to move is because we believe it's in their best interest; our interest will be served if they win. Here are some thoughts on stimulating movement:

## Stimulating with Hard Evidence

We want to hold out some data and get their reaction. We wouldn't show it to them unless we thought it signaled a problem or result worth addressing. We don't know if they will agree, so we ask. For example:

"In working with your people, we ran across the fact that you have a 40 percent turnover in your first-year engineering staff. Typically, that would raise a red flag. *How do you feel about that number?*"

If they don't like that number we can ask:

"*What would you like it to be?*" (Or "What should it be?" "What do you need it to be?")

"*What is the value of the difference?*" (Between present number and future number, what is the dollar value of the difference?)

"*If we had some thoughts on how you could move from X to Y, should we be talking?*"

Note the last question. I said before that we should have an end in

mind for every interaction with the client. We should know what we want them to say, do, or decide. At the end of this conversation, they should be able to say and decide the following:

- This is worth pursuing. (Begin collaboration.)
- Thanks, but I'm not interested. (Great. What *are* the key concerns you're facing?)

I was working with a company that trained trainers to teach their material. They felt they could leverage their impact and empower others. I ran across the fact that people who trained in their program (for five days) only gave an average of .8 in-house sessions in one year's time in the sponsoring company. This did not seem to be a good number for either party. I found the person who would care about this number and asked him how he felt about it. He said it was horrible. I asked him what he'd like it to be. He said about 5. We calculated the value of the difference, and it was big bucks. I asked, "If I had some ideas on how you could move from .8 to 5, should we be talking?"

Another client gave quarterly reports to all their clients. Each report included recommendations. We found some hard data that said only 1 in 10 recommendations was ever acted upon. We asked the person who cared how he felt about that number. He thought it should be at least 3. The value of the difference was big. We decided to spend some mutual effort on how they could get from 1 to 3. And so it goes.

## Stimulating with Soft Evidence

This is not necessarily as compelling as hard data. It can still get us started. We talk to a small sample of people who have some evidence of a problem or desired result, or we do a small survey, perhaps statistically insignificant, yet indicative. We bring it to the client to get a reaction. For example:

"We talked to four of your managers, and they all said they didn't have sufficient information to make key decisions. If all of your managers felt that way, would it be a problem?"

If the answer is yes, then we would like to know, "What is the likelihood that these four are not the only ones who feel this way?" They will either say, "Very likely," "I don't know," or "Those are the only four." If it is very likely, we can proceed to impact. If they don't know, we can suggest a diagnostic. If they are the only four—is that a problem?

Sample surveys can be a powerful form of soft evidence, perhaps even turning to hard data. One of my former colleagues was working with a large corporation complaining of "communication problems." When he peeled the onion, they said they were spending too much time on reports. He created and conducted a simple survey and gave it to 20 of their 300 supervisors. It showed they were spending, on the average, 15 hours a week dealing with reports in one way or another. He was introduced to the person who would care, and submitted his soft

evidence. Basically he said, "How do you feel about that number?" The executive said it should be more like five to six hours a week. The value of the difference was huge. The next step was a diagnostic to find out if the sample held true for the larger audience, and if so, what were the contributing factors. That led to a much larger project.

## Stimulating with Presumed Evidence

We can offer the client data from third-party sources and get their reaction. The numbers may or may not apply to their company; we won't know if we don't ask. For example:

"A study I just read said that 14 percent of executives' time is wasted on poor communication between management and staff. What do you think a similar percentage is here?" Whatever they say, we can ask, "And how do you feel about that number?" We would then proceed as with hard evidence.

Another example: "The Gartner Group estimates that 70 percent of IT projects fail to produce the expected benefits because the IT processes are not integrated into work processes. What's your sense—is that a possibility with some of the projects here?"

## Stimulating with a Solution

We could also approach the client directly with the latest and greatest hot, new solution. Rather than get bogged down in features and benefits, we can give them a brief sense of what it does and why it is so hot. We can then move off our own solution. For example:

- "Of course, the only reason people are excited is because it's solving these kinds of problems. Are any of these things problems? How so?"

- "Of course, the only reason people are so excited is because it's producing these kinds of results. Are these results the kind of results you're interested in?"

## Notice Where We Are

We haven't pushed any solutions on the client that they don't need or aren't interested in. In fact, we only moved to a solution once we found a problem worth solving or a result worth producing. We didn't guess—we asked. And we did our homework. We took the time to research. We understood their business, perhaps even better than they. The worst that could happen is they thank us for our interest and effort, yet don't feel the need to "move." They have other issues that are more pressing. Great! What are they? Can they solve them on their own, or would they like some help?

Yes, this process is more work, not so much physically as intellectually. It is also more effective. It helps sustain and extend long-term relationships.

## Continue the Collaboration

Once we have the green light to pursue the opportunity, we work with our counterparts to build a strong business case (evidence, impact, context, constraints) for which we can attract resources (time,

people, money) and develop a decision process. The client will know better than we about how to do these things. We may know better than they about how to create ORDER. If we collaborate, we should be able to present an exact solution to people who decide, and have a high probability of success.

## Access to People Who Decide

One last thought. Getting immediate access to a high-level decision maker can be effective for a pull strategy. We start on their agenda. For a push strategy, premature access to a decision maker can be deadly. If we walk in with only features and benefits of our great solution, and find a lack of interest and enthusiasm, we have blown a rare opportunity. We may never get that access again. For a push strategy, we may be better served by collaborating with *people who care* to build a tight business rationale before we arrive at the decision maker's door.

**Helping *Current* Clients Succeed**

# 26
# The Last Word

We can do this. It is possible, practical, and productive to focus our business development efforts on helping clients succeed. The more we increase the success of others, the more successful we will be. Intense global competition and radically enhanced worldwide communication will ensure that those who help clients succeed will be rewarded, and those who don't will be penalized. Both the rewards and penalties are great.

Individuals and organizations changing their paradigm from selling to succeeding—from dysfunctional practices to mutual success and satisfaction—bring new skill sets to the business development dialogue. Those with a high emotional quotient will be rewarded with superior information about true needs, resources, and decision criteria. With an applied intelligence quotient, they will build better business cases for proposed interventions, make astute systemic connections, and

push innovation and creative thinking to new levels. Conversely, those wed to twentieth-century selling models will be penalized with inferior communication, wasted efforts, and less probability of finding meaningful, relevant solutions.

Helping clients succeed is a way of engaging the world. I find it energizing and deeply rewarding on many levels. It allows me to absorb knowledge and skills from diverse arenas and apply them in daily interactions. By "walking my talk" and applying what I learn, I never stop growing in awareness and choice. I welcome your company on that journey, and look forward to learning from your unique experience.

# Appendix A

## Client Profile

Date _____

Client Name _____

Organization _____

Opportunity _____

**Account Information**

Address _____   Phone _____

City _____   Fax _____

State _____ ZIP _____   Cell _____

E-mail _____   Home _____


Assistant _____   Assistant Phone _____

**Organizational Role** _____

**Buying Role**

☐ Decision Maker   ☐ Gatekeeper   ☐ Influencer   ☐ Champion   ☐ User   ☐ _____

**Organizational Context (The Big Picture)**

_____
_____
_____
_____
_____
_____
_____

**Necessary Data**

_____
_____
_____
_____
_____
_____

**BUSINESS OPPORTUNITY WORKSHEET**

Who and what else is affected?

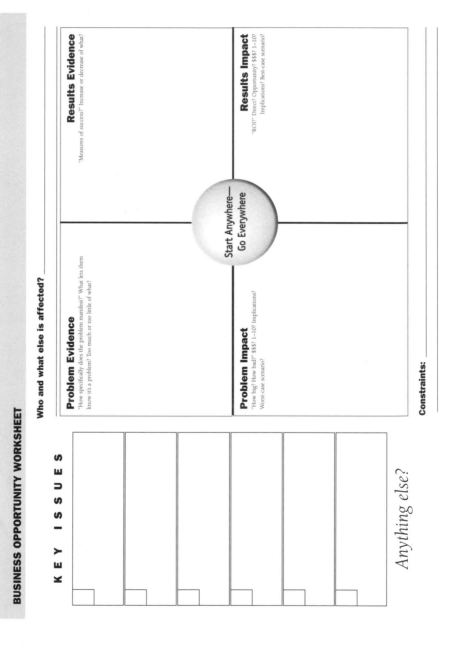

**Problem Evidence**

"How specifically does the problem manifest?" What lets them know it's a problem? Too much or too little of what?

**Results Evidence**

"Measures of success?" Increase or decrease of what?

Start Anywhere—
Go Everywhere

**Problem Impact**

"How big? How bad?" $$$? 1–10? Implications? Worst-case scenario?

**Results Impact**

"ROI?" Direct? Opportunity? $$$? 1–10? Implications? Best-case scenario?

Constraints:

**K E Y   I S S U E S**

*Anything else?*

## BUSINESS OPPORTUNITY WORKSHEET

### ISSUE 2

| Problem Evidence | Results Evidence |
|---|---|
| Problem Impact | Results Impact |

Constraints:

### ISSUE 3

| Problem Evidence | Results Evidence |
|---|---|
| Problem Impact | Results Impact |

Constraints:

## RESOURCES

**Time:**

**People:**

**Money:** Agreed upon range?

## THE DECISION PROCESS

| Steps | Decision | When | Who | How |
|---|---|---|---|---|
| | | | | Capture this person's criteria below. Fill out a seperate profile for each key decision maker and influencer. |
| | | | | |
| | | | | |
| | | | | |
| | | | | |

**The Competition?**

**Gain/Loss**

**Personal Stake**

**Decision Criteria**

**Personal Belief:** If it were up to this person to make the final decision, what would he or she do?

# Appendix B

## Proactive Approach to Understanding Client Needs

Account Development Worksheet

**Client:**

| Problem/Result | Evidence | |
|---|---|---|
| | Type<br>H=Hard<br>S=Soft<br>P=Presumed | Source<br>(What, Where, Who) |
| | | |
| | | |
| | | |
| | | |
| | | |
| | | |
| | | |
| | | |
| | | |
| | | |
| | | |
| | | |
| | | |
| | | |
| | | |
| | | |
| | | |
| | | |
| | | |

Account Development Worksheet

**Proposed Solution:** _____

| Impact | Constraints | People Who Care |
|--------|-------------|-----------------|
|        |             |                 |
|        |             |                 |
|        |             |                 |
|        |             |                 |
|        |             |                 |
|        |             |                 |
|        |             |                 |
|        |             |                 |
|        |             |                 |
|        |             |                 |
|        |             |                 |
|        |             |                 |
|        |             |                 |
|        |             |                 |
|        |             |                 |
|        |             |                 |
|        |             |                 |
|        |             |                 |

## About the Author

Mahan Khalsa is a world-renowned consultant in business development. He graduated with honors in economics from UCLA, and has an M.B.A. from Harvard Business School. A consultant to *Fortune 500* companies, the hallmarks of Mahan are insight, respect, intellect, and a pragmatic approach to selling and business development. He is an expert in global best practices of consulting and business development, and has applied those findings to some of the world's largest and most successful organizations. Mahan is also author of the book *Asking Effective Questions*.

## About Franklin Covey

Our mission: "We inspire change by igniting the power of proven principles so that people and organizations achieve what matters most." Franklin Covey is an international professional services and leadership development firm dedicated to increasing the effectiveness of individuals and organizations. Effectiveness is the ability to get results now in a way that increases your ability to produce results in the future. We provide professional services and products in the following five areas:

- Consulting
- Assessment and measurement
- Training and education
- Implementation processes
- Application tools and products

A partial list of Franklin Covey training and education programs include:

Helping Clients Succeed™

The 7 Habits of Highly Effective People®

What Matters Most® (using the Franklin Planner™)

The 4 Roles of Leadership™

The Organizational Effectiveness Cycle™

Presentation Advantage™

Writing Advantage®

Franklin Covey Project Management™

Franklin Covey comprises a powerful diversity of professional skills, talents, and experience. Our extensive client base includes thousands of business, government, and educational organizations, as well as millions of individual customers.

## About the Sales Performance Group at Franklin Covey

Our mission: "To inspire change in the way people interact in developing business by helping clients and consultants create mutual success and satisfaction in achieving what matters most." The Sales Performance Group is introducing a fresh, unique approach to business development. *Helping Clients Succeed*™ is the training program based on the book *Let's Get Real or Let's Not Play*. This workshop will help your sales force and consultants transcend traditional selling to develop lasting relationships, recognize and create high-leverage opportunities, drive down the cost of sales, and learn to enjoy selling again. Get to what's real for your clients—call the Franklin Covey Sales Performance Group at 1-800-707-5191 for more information about our training just for sales professionals and consultants.